Automating Microsoft Azure Infrastructure Services

Michael Washam

Beijing · Cambridge · Farnham · Köln · Sebastopol · Tokyo

Automating Microsoft Azure Infrastructure Services

by Michael Washam

Copyright © 2015 Opsgility, LLC. All rights reserved.

Printed in the United States of America.

Published by O'Reilly Media, Inc., 1005 Gravenstein Highway North, Sebastopol, CA 95472.

O'Reilly books may be purchased for educational, business, or sales promotional use. Online editions are also available for most titles (*http://safaribooksonline.com*). For more information, contact our corporate/institutional sales department: 800-998-9938 or *corporate@oreilly.com*.

Editors: Rachel Roumeliotis and Allyson MacDonald	**Indexer:** Wendy Catalano
Production Editor: Matthew Hacker	**Cover Designer:** Ellie Volckhausen
Copyeditor: Sonia Saruba	**Interior Designer:** David Futato
Proofreader: Sharon Wilkey	**Illustrator:** Rebecca Demarest

November 2014:   First Edition

Revision History for the First Edition:

2014-10-17:   First release

See *http://oreilly.com/catalog/errata.csp?isbn=9781491944899* for release details.

ISBN: 978-1-491-94489-9

[LSI]

Table of Contents

Foreword

Based on the fact that you're reading this, you are probably already convinced that the cloud offers agility and elasticity unmatchable by traditional IT infrastructure. Using a cloud's infrastructure service APIs, whether via a portal, a REST client, or scripts, you can create virtual machines (VMs) in minutes instead of days or hours, configure those VMs with secure network connectivity to each other and external networks, and then shut them down, paying only for the time that they were active and you were using them. The scenarios unlocked by this new self-service model are disrupting the computing landscape and causing a rush toward the cloud.

Coincident with the cloud-computing disruption is the DevOps revolution. Just as cloud vendors like Microsoft Azure must fully automate their infrastructure in order to scale to millions of servers, efficient DevOps at even modest scale also requires automation. Using a portal to by-hand re-create your production environment for dev/test deployments of your latest updates is onerous, time-consuming, and error-prone. Similarly, scaling out your front-ends in response to a load spike isn't something that you want to be ready to respond to at any time of day or night, whenever your application's load exceeds its provisioned capacity. Automation is therefore key to realizing the full potential of the cloud.

While there are numerous tools, scripting engines, and even full-featured products designed to enable automation, PowerShell has set the gold standard for Windows automation. All of Microsoft's enterprise products are built on a foundation of PowerShell management, and Microsoft Azure is no exception. With its consistent syntax, rich grammar, built-in verbs, and object pipeline, PowerShell scripts have the expressiveness of compiled languages and compositional capabilities that bring object-oriented programming to scripting like text pipelining never can. With PowerShell at your command, you can script Microsoft Azure IaaS VM environments to create reproducible yet complex deployments, scale up and down tiers, perform automated failure recovery, and more.

There's no one more qualified to teach you how to make the most of PowerShell with Microsoft Azure IaaS VMs than Michael. I worked with him closely when he was at Microsoft, both when he was on the Developer and Platform Evangelism team contributing PowerShell scripts for managing Microsoft Azure, and then when he joined the Microsoft Azure team to continue his work. In fact, he helped design and set up my demos for the TechEd North America 2012 keynote address, which served as the launch event for Microsoft Azure's Infrastructure Services preview release. Not surprisingly, the keynote demo deployment and reset system was built with the original Infrastructure Services PowerShell cmdlets.

This book is the definitive overview and deep reference on using Microsoft Azure's PowerShell cmdlets to automate Microsoft Azure Infrastructure Services. Whether you're launching basic VMs, configuring ExpressRoute network connections, or standing up full SharePoint farms, Michael's expert guidance will show you how easy it is to automate your way to the full potential of DevOps and agility on Microsoft Azure.

—Mark Russinovich
Chief technical officer, Microsoft Azure, Microsoft

Preface

Who This Book Is For

This book is for the IT professional or developer who has been tasked with deploying workloads in Azure. At some point in your project(s), either you will be required to use PowerShell or the temptation to finally dive into automation will pull you in this direction. This book does assume that the reader has some experience with PowerShell or scripting in general and has previous experience with Microsoft Azure. Of course, there are plenty of resources on the Internet and other books from this publisher that can help guide you on the way if you lack experience in either topic.

What This Book Is About

This book is about automating and configuring Microsoft Azure Virtual Machines and Virtual Networks by using the Azure PowerShell cmdlets.

Overview of Chapters

- Chapter 1, *Introduction*, provides some background on where the Azure cmdlets came from and some insight into why automation in the cloud is critical.

- Chapter 2, *Getting Started with Azure PowerShell*, is about getting up and running with the Azure cmdlets, from installation to the configuration of your Azure subscription.

- Chapter 3, *Virtual Machines*, jumps right into creating and updating virtual machines in PowerShell.

- Chapter 4, *Virtual Machine Networking*, includes topic such as reserved IPs, ACLs, external load balancing, and network endpoints.

- Chapter 5, *Virtual Machine Storage*, is focused on storage as it relates to virtual machines. Topics such as images and disks, and uploading and copying virtual hard disks (VHDs) are covered in depth.

- Chapter 6, *Virtual Networks*, takes the reader through automating virtual networks and discusses other related topics such as static IPs and the internal load-balancer.

- Chapter 7, *Advanced Virtual Machines*, discusses more-advanced topics such as the provisioning engine, using virtual machine extensions, and the import and export cmdlets in conjunction with the async blob copy API.

Conventions Used in This Book

The following typographical conventions are used in this book:

Italic
> Indicates new terms, URLs, email addresses, filenames, and file extensions.

`Constant width`
> Used for program listings, as well as within paragraphs to refer to program elements such as variable or function names, databases, data types, environment variables, statements, and keywords.

`Constant width bold`
> Shows commands or other text that should be typed literally by the user.

`Constant width italic`
> Shows text that should be replaced with user-supplied values or by values determined by context.

 This icon signifies a tip, suggestion, or general note.

 This icon indicates a warning or caution.

Using Code Examples

This book is here to help you get your job done. In general, if example code is offered with this book, you may use it in your programs and documentation. You do not need to contact us for permission unless you're reproducing a significant portion of the code. For example, writing a program that uses several chunks of code from this book does not require permission. Selling or distributing a CD-ROM of examples from O'Reilly books does require permission. Answering a question by citing this book and quoting example code does not require permission. Incorporating a significant amount of example code from this book into your product's documentation does require permission.

We appreciate, but do not require, attribution. An attribution usually includes the title, author, publisher, and ISBN. For example: "*Automating Microsoft Azure Infrastructure Services* by Michael Washam (O'Reilly). Copyright 2015 Opsgility, LLC, 978-1-491-94489-9."

If you feel your use of code examples falls outside fair use or the permission given above, feel free to contact us at *permissions@oreilly.com*.

Safari® Books Online

 *Safari Books Online* is an on-demand digital library that delivers expert content in both book and video form from the world's leading authors in technology and business.

Technology professionals, software developers, web designers, and business and creative professionals use Safari Books Online as their primary resource for research, problem solving, learning, and certification training.

Safari Books Online offers a range of product mixes and pricing programs for organizations, government agencies, and individuals. Subscribers have access to thousands of books, training videos, and prepublication manuscripts in one fully searchable database from publishers like O'Reilly Media, Prentice Hall Professional, Addison-Wesley Professional, Microsoft Press, Sams, Que, Peachpit Press, Focal Press, Cisco Press, John Wiley & Sons, Syngress, Morgan Kaufmann, IBM Redbooks, Packt, Adobe Press, FT Press, Apress, Manning, New Riders, McGraw-Hill, Jones & Bartlett, Course Technology, and dozens more. For more information about Safari Books Online, please visit us online.

How to Contact Us

Please address comments and questions concerning this book to the publisher:

O'Reilly Media, Inc.
1005 Gravenstein Highway North
Sebastopol, CA 95472
800-998-9938 (in the United States or Canada)
707-829-0515 (international or local)
707-829-0104 (fax)

We have a web page for this book, where we list errata, examples, and any additional information. You can access this page at *http://bit.ly/automating_azure_infrastructure*.

To comment or ask technical questions about this book, send email to *bookques tions@oreilly.com*.

For more information about our books, courses, conferences, and news, see our website at *http://www.oreilly.com*.

Find us on Facebook: *http://facebook.com/oreilly*

Follow us on Twitter: *http://twitter.com/oreillymedia*

Watch us on YouTube: *http://www.youtube.com/oreillymedia*

Acknowledgments

Writing this book has been a fantastic experience. I have learned so much about what it takes to make a coherent piece of writing (at least I hope I did), and I owe a lot to the people who pushed me through this with encouragement and just incredible hard work.

First of all, I would like to thank my wife for encouraging me to do this, and also for her and my children putting up with me during its completion.

Second, I would like to thank my editors at O'Reilly, Rachel Roumeliotis and Allyson MacDonald, for taking on this project and helping me through it.

Finally, I would like to thank my technical reviewers, who walked through the book multiple times with a fine-tooth comb and gave incredibly useful feedback:

- Aleksandar Nikolic—PowerShell MVP—*http://www.powershellmagazine.com*
- Michael Collier—Microsoft Azure MVP—*http://michaelcollier.wordpress.com*
- David Moravec—PowerShell MVP—*http://powershell.cz*

It has been fantastic working with all three of you, and I hope we can do this again!

## CHAPTER 1

Introduction

The Microsoft Azure PowerShell cmdlets are one of the primary tools in use today for automating Microsoft Azure from the Windows platform. The cmdlets take the native automation capabilities of PowerShell and add in the ability to provision compute and other services on the fly in Microsoft Azure. This mix of technical capabilities has truly opened the doors to cloud automation in Microsoft Azure, providing the ability to deploy solutions that are both complex and at scale.

Why Use the Microsoft Azure PowerShell Cmdlets?

Prior to the dawn of cloud computing, deploying a new application was a fairly involved task. First, you had to order servers, wait for them to ship, unpack them from their boxes, set up the network, install an operating system, patch the operating system, and finally install software and configure your application. I am purposely glossing over the "organizational agility" needed to accomplish this if you were responsible for the application but another group was responsible for the infrastructure.

Thanks to cloud providers such as Microsoft and Amazon, you as the lucky individual living in the cloud-computing era can now skip many of these steps and focus on managing your application or infrastructure at a much higher level. The cloud removes the responsibility from you to manage hardware resources directly. Now it can be as easy as clicking through a web page-based wizard to provision numerous virtual machines and then logging in to deploy and configure your application. This is definitely a huge improvement in infrastructure and application management.

However, the cloud does more than give you the ability to spin up virtual machines from a web page. It also gives you the ability to treat virtual machines and other services as programmable resources. To show why this is important, I want to compare deploying the same application using three different techniques.

Comparing Deployment Methods

Deploying an Application in a Traditional Data Center

1. Order server and networking hardware.
2. Wait for hardware to ship.
3. Install and configure networking hardware.
4. Install and configure server hardware (apply firmware updates as needed).
5. Install a base operating system on the server hardware.
6. Patch the base operating system.
7. Install software applications and roles.
8. Deploy applications.
9. Repeat steps 3 through 8 (and likely steps 1 and 2, depending on how accurate the initial planning was) for staging, development, and testing environments.

Deploying an Application in the Cloud (Without Automation)

1. Launch the management portal.
2. Create and configure each virtual machine.
3. Patch the base operating system.
4. Install software applications and roles.
5. Deploy applications.
6. Repeat steps 2 through 5 for staging, development, and testing environments.

Deploying an Application in the Cloud (with Automation)

1. Identify repeatable processes.
2. Create automation configuration and scripts for step 1.
3. Deploy scripts for application.
4. Repeat step 3 for staging, development, and testing environments.

Comparing the methods, you can see that with the cloud, your return on investment with automation is measured in agility. If your organization can benefit from an agile approach to infrastructure deployment and management, where you can quickly spin up and tear down computing envionments, then you are probably reading the right book.

History

The Microsoft Azure PowerShell cmdlets started as two distinct projects. The first was an official product created by one of the engineering teams to create a set of scaffolding cmdlets that allowed Windows users to create Node.js applications that could run as a Microsoft Azure cloud service. The second set of cmdlets were created over the years by various technical evangelists (including myself) in the Microsoft Developer and Platform Evangelism (DPE) team.

The cmdlets built by the evangelism team at first covered only the basics of creating and deploying cloud services and were built specifically for two purposes:

- Automate the creation and deployment of demos for evangelism efforts
- Serve as source code samples to demonstrate the Microsoft Azure Service Management API

When I joined the Microsoft Azure evangelism team, one of the projects I took over was the PowerShell cmdlets. Working with a few solid developers, we started slowly adding new functionality as time and budget permitted. I came from a background of troubleshooting and debugging, so one of the very first areas we improved was the diagnostics cmdlets for cloud services (sadly, these did not see the light in the official release). After diagnostics, we added support for SQL Database (known as SQL Azure at the time), then Traffic Manager, and finally the last major work in evangelism was the cmdlets for Microsoft Azure Infrastructure Services.

With the eminent launch of Microsoft Azure Infrastructure Services, the engineering team became very interested in the cmdlets and worked very closely with us on identifying the capabilities and answering questions that came up during development. When the initial cmdlets were complete, the integration work with the engineering team that owned the Node.js cmdlets merged what was a code sample and a set of cmdlets built for developers into what would be the first release of the Microsoft Azure PowerShell cmdlets.

A year after the intial launch of the cmdlets, I joined the Microsoft Azure runtime team as a senior program manager and worked with some amazing developers and testers to add much more functionality to the original cmdlets that I helped initially build. In addition to this core team that handled virtual machines, cloud services, and the core Service Management API, Microsoft now has several teams for various services. These teams are focused on making a great automation experience for Microsoft Azure via PowerShell as well as command-line tools that run natively on Mac and Linux. The cmdlets have grown at such a rapid pace that this book is focused only on the subset related directly to infrastructure services.

Open Source

Like most of the SDKs and tools for Microsoft Azure, the PowerShell cmdlets are completely open source and licensed under the Apache 2.0 license. The source is hosted in a GitHub repository located at *https://github.com/Azure/azure-sdk-tools*. Feel free to fork or clone the repository, file bugs, or even submit changes back to the cmdlets. If you would like to contribute, there is a page that describes the agreements needed that I would highly recommend as your first step: *http://azure.github.io/guidelines*.

Summary

Now that you know why automation in the cloud is important and have a little background on how the Microsoft Azure PowerShell cmdlets came to life, let's dive right in. The only thing you will need going forward is a Microsoft Azure account.

## CHAPTER 2

Getting Started with Azure PowerShell

Installation

The Microsoft Azure PowerShell cmdlets are officially supported on Windows 2008 R2, Windows 7, Windows 8/8.1, and Server 2012/2012 R2. Assuming you are running one of these operating systems (and likely later operating systems) and at least PowerShell 3.0, launch your browser and go to the Microsoft Azure home page at *http://azure.micro soft.com*. From there, click the Downloads link on the page; you will then see another menu for the various download types available. You, of course, are a PowerShell user, so you will want to click the link for Command Line Tools.

The installation can take several minutes because there is a dependency on the Microsoft Azure SDK, which has its own set of dependencies. For a leaner installation, the Azure PowerShell cmdlets also come as a standalone install. You can install the standalone version by going directly to the GitHub repository at *http://bit.ly/azure-sdk-tools*.

Setting Up Your Environment

When the installation for the cmdlets is complete, you can choose your method of running them. You can launch PowerShell either by clicking the PowerShell icon on your computer or by running *powershell.exe*. Another alternative is running a more interactive editor that provides features such as IntelliSense and code snippets. My preference is the latter, and the editor I will use going forward in this book is the PowerShell Integrated Scripting Environment (ISE). In Windows 7 and above, the PowerShell ISE is installed by default, and all that is required is to run *powershell_ise.exe*.

Launch the PowerShell ISE and click the small arrow at the top right of the console. This will open the Script pane, where you can type PowerShell commands and save it as a separate script file.

Authenticating to Microsoft Azure

You have two choices for authenticating to Microsoft Azure from PowerShell. You can use your Microsoft Azure username and password with support for a Microsoft or an Organization account in the Azure Active Directory, or you can use certificate-based authentication.

Authenticating with a certificate

The easiest way to get started with certificate authentication is to download a *.publish-settings* file from Microsoft Azure by using the `Get-AzurePublishSettingsFile` cmdlet. This cmdlet launches the default browser and takes you to a page on the Microsoft Azure site where you can log in with a Microsoft or Organization account that has access to your Microsoft Azure subscription. When you have successfully logged in, you will be prompted to select a subscription if your account has access to more than one and then prompted to download a *.publishsettings* file.

To execute, press F5, or highlight the call to the `Get-AzurePublishSettingsFile` cmdlet in the editor and press F8 (see Figure 2-1).

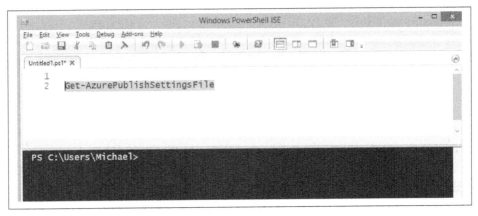

Figure 2-1. Executing Get-AzurePublishSettingsFile

About the .publishsettings file

The file you download should be treated with care. In the file is the name of your subscription, subscription ID, and a newly-generated management certificate that allows you to access the subscription. Whoever has access to this file has access to your subscription. Microsoft Azure imposes a limit on the total number of management certificates that can be associated with a subscription at any given time.

At the time of this writing, the maximum number of certificates is 100. Each time you run the `Get-AzurePublishSettingsFile` cmdlet, Microsoft Azure generates a new management certificate in the subscription you choose. If there are multiple users on a subscription, you should develop a certificate management strategy early on to avoid problems later.

Importing the .publishsettings file

The next step in configuring the Microsoft Azure PowerShell cmdlets is importing the previously downloaded *.publishsettings* file. As I mentioned earlier, this file contains a management certificate that allows access to your Microsoft Azure subscription. The cmdlets use this certificate for authentication to the Service Management API.

To import, simply add a call to `Import-AzurePublishSettingsFile` and pass to it the path to the previously downloaded file (see Figure 2-2). Press F5, or highlight the text and press F8.

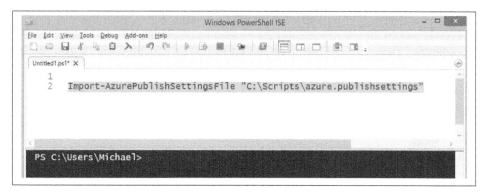

Figure 2-2. Importing a .publishsettings file

Using Microsoft Azure AD to authenticate with PowerShell

An alternative method to using certificates is to authenticate using an account from the Microsoft Azure Active Directory. Each new Microsoft Azure subscription will have its own Active Directory tenant by default. From a PowerShell perspective, this means that you are not required to use management certificates to authenticate and access your subscription.

Using the `Add-AzureAccount` cmdlet, you can specify the username and password of a user who has administrative or co-administrative rights on your subscription, and use the returned token to execute PowerShell commands with your subscription (see Figure 2-3).

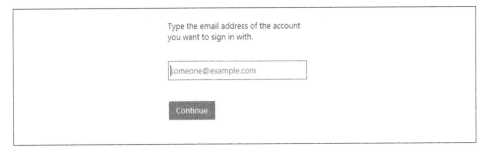

Figure 2-3. Using Add-AzureAccount to authenticate

The token returned from Add-AzureAccount is valid for up to 12 hours. After the token expires, you will need to authenticate again by running Add-AzureAccount and entering your username and password. This is not ideal for scripts that need to run in a purely automated fashion without user intervention of any kind. For noninteractive scripts, the Add-AzureAccount cmdlet supports passing a PSCredential object to the -Credential parameter. At the moment, this support works only with organizational accounts.

Switching back to certificate authentication

When you use the Add-AzureAccount cmdlet, all of your subscriptions for that account will be modified to use Azure AD authentication. If you want to switch back to using certificates, you will have to remove the account settings first by calling Remove-AzureAccount.

Managing Subscriptions

Once you have downloaded and imported your subscription settings (or authenticated using your username and password), there are several other cmdlets you should be aware of that are involved with managing your subscription settings in PowerShell.

Get-AzureSubscription

The Get-AzureSubscription cmdlet returns and enumerates subscriptions that have been imported or manually configured with the Set-AzureSubscription cmdlet. These settings are persisted in the *$env:APPDATA\Windows Azure PowerShell* folder.

Get-AzureSubscription also supports the parameters listed in Table 2-1 to help you identify subscription settings.

Table 2-1. Get-AzureSubscription parameters

-Default	Returns the default subscription. When you start a new PowerShell session, this will be the subscription used if no other subscription is selected.
-Current	Returns the currently selected subscription.

-ExtendedDetails   Returns quota details for the current or specified subscription.

The -ExtendedDetails parameter is especially useful for ensuring that you have enough quota available in your subscription for whatever operation you are automating (see Figure 2-4).

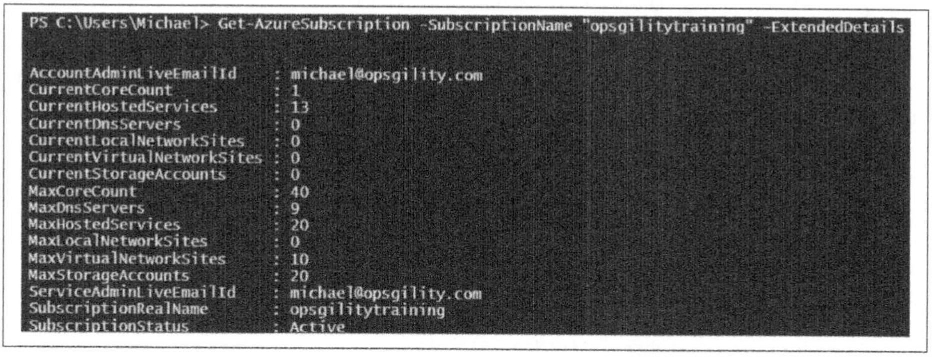

```
PS C:\Users\Michael> Get-AzureSubscription -SubscriptionName "opsgilitytraining" -ExtendedDetails

AccountAdminLiveEmailId        : michael@opsgility.com
CurrentCoreCount               : 1
CurrentHostedServices          : 13
CurrentDnsServers              : 0
CurrentLocalNetworkSites       : 0
CurrentVirtualNetworkSites     : 0
CurrentStorageAccounts         : 0
MaxCoreCount                   : 40
MaxDnsServers                  : 9
MaxHostedServices              : 20
MaxLocalNetworkSites           : 0
MaxVirtualNetworkSites         : 10
MaxStorageAccounts             : 20
ServiceAdminLiveEmailId        : michael@opsgility.com
SubscriptionRealName           : opsgilitytraining
SubscriptionStatus             : Active
```

Figure 2-4. Viewing quota information with Get-AzureSubscription

Select-AzureSubscription

At runtime, the cmdlets have a concept of the current subscription selected in your PowerShell session. This functionality allows you to execute scripts using multiple subscriptions. For instance, you could write a script that enumerates all of your subscriptions and deletes unused disks in each of them or stops all virtual machines. The cmdlet to switch between subscriptions is Select-AzureSubscription (see Example 2-1). Simply call the cmdlet with the subscription name you want to work on, and any new calls to Azure will use this subscription.

Example 2-1. Switching between multiple subscriptions

```
Select-AzureSubscription "[subscription one name]"

Get-AzureVM    # returns the status of all VMs in subscription one

Select-AzureSubscription "[subscription two name]"

Get-AzureVM    # returns the status of all VMs in subscription two
```

This cmdlet can also be used to change the current and default subscriptions for your PowerShell sessions with the parameters in Table 2-2.

Table 2-2. Select-AzureSubscription parameters

-Default	Changes the subscription specified to be the new default subscription for all PowerShell sessions.
-Current	Changes the subscription specified to be the new current subscription for the active PowerShell session.

-NoDefault   Clears the default subscription settings from all PowerShell sessions.

-NoCurrent   Clears the current subscription settings from the active PowerShell session.

Set-AzureSubscription

The `Set-AzureSubscription` cmdlet allows you to add a subscription to the stored settings or change properties on an existing subscription.

Example 2-2 shows how to associate a manually created certificate and associate it with a Microsoft Azure subscription. The same call could be used to modify an existing subscription by changing the certificate associated with the subscription.

Example 2-2. Manually configuring a Microsoft Azure subscription

```
$cert = Get-Item Cert:\CurrentUser\My\[certificate thumbprint]

$subscriptionID = "[your subscription ID]"
$localName = "[manually added subscription name]"

Set-AzureSubscription -SubscriptionName $localName `
                      -SubscriptionId $subscriptionID `
                      -Certificate $cert
```

Manually creating and uploading management certificates
If you would like to manually create and manage management certificates, simply use the *makecert.exe* utility as documented in MSDN *http://bit.ly/use_makecert_utility* and upload the certificate through the management portal. You can also view the certificate thumbprint in the portal user interface.

Just as you can add and update a subscription, you can also remove the subscription from your local PowerShell configuration by calling the `Remove-AzureSubscription` cmdlet (see Example 2-3).

Example 2-3. Removing a Microsoft Azure subscription

```
$subscriptionName = "[subscription name]"

Remove-AzureSubscription -SubscriptionName $subscriptionName
```

Executing Scripts in This Book

It may take several lines of script when using the Microsoft Azure PowerShell cmdlets to execute a task. During these times, I find it is simpler to add the lines to a single script and use the PowerShell ISE to execute the entire script at once (see Figure 2-5).

Other times you may want simple environment information from Microsoft Azure such as the name of the available regions or a list of storage account names in your

---

subscription. For these one-line operations, I prefer to execute the scripts using the PowerShell console (the Console pane of the PowerShell ISE works well too) and then use the values within the script that I am building.

Throughout this book are examples that I recommend you try as learning exercises and others that are just for reference. In the learning exercises, I will note when I am using the Console pane to execute a command and when I am building a new script by noting that the code should go in the Script pane (see Figure 2-5). You may, of course, do this however you like, but if you are new to PowerShell, I hope these tips will help guide you along the examples throughout the book.

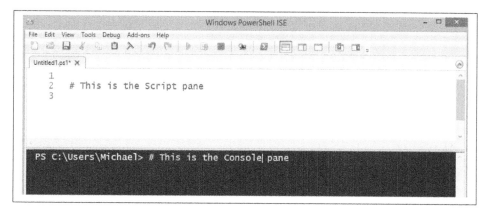

Figure 2-5. The PowerShell ISE

 Executing script with F5 versus F8 in the PowerShell ISE Script pane
As you progress through the book, you will be asked to execute code in several ways. Within the Script pane are two primary methods that you will use in this book. Pressing F5 in the Script pane executes the entire script that is loaded. Pressing F8 executes only the script code that is currently selected or the line that the cursor is on. Sometimes you should execute the entire script with F5 and sometimes only the selected portion with F8.

Summary

In this chapter we have seen where to download the cmdlets from and how to configure one or more Microsoft Azure subscriptions. In Chapter 3 we will dive right into doing something useful with the cmdlets, starting with creating and configuring virtual machines.

Virtual Machines

Creating Virtual Machines with PowerShell

In this chapter you will learn about using the Microsoft Azure PowerShell cmdlets to create a virtual machine with Microsoft Azure platform images. As part of learning this process, you will learn how to specify the initial configuration settings such as the local administrator account name and password, the virtual machine size (CPUs and memory), network endpoints, and underlying storage. From there you will learn how to use those same concepts to modify the configuration of existing virtual machines, whether they are running or not.

To get started creating your first virtual machine using PowerShell, you will need some environment information from Microsoft Azure. This is the same information that you use in the portal, such as the region name and the storage account that will be used as the location where your virtual machine disks are created.

For the first part of this chapter, I would recommend creating a new PowerShell file and saving it with a name such as *chapter3create.ps1*. Some portions of this chapter will be saved to the script and edited in the Script pane (top portion of the ISE) to make it easier to follow, and some portions should be executed in the Console pane (bottom portion of the ISE) for immediate results.

The first call related to Microsoft Azure of your new script should always be to `Select-AzureSubscription` to ensure that you are executing commands against the correct Microsoft Azure subscription.

Add the code shown in Example 3-1 to create a variable to store your subscription name and then select that subscription for use. Ensure that you replace the placeholder values with real ones.

Example 3-1. Selecting your subscription (Script pane)

```
$subscription = "[subscription name]"

Select-AzureSubscription $subscription
```

Replacing the subscription name placeholder
Remember, you can find the name of your subscriptions by calling `Get-AzureSubscription | Select SubscriptionName` in the Console pane. Use that value instead of the placeholder value in the example. The subscription name is case sensitive!

Executing the script

When the call to `Select-AzureSubscription` is in place, press F5, or highlight the script and press F8, to select your current subscription. This will validate that you have the correct subscription name in place and will also set any future commands run from the Console pane to that subscription.

Virtual Machine Location and Storage

All resources in Microsoft Azure are created in a specific region. This is the same region that you see in the management portal when you create a virtual machine.

To retrieve a list of available regions, you can run the `Get-AzureLocation` cmdlet (see Example 3-2). Since the goal is to have an immediate list of available names and not run these each time you execute this script, I would suggest you run this command in the Console pane of the PowerShell ISE (see Example 3-2).

Example 3-2. Returning Microsoft Azure location details (Console pane)

```
Get-AzureLocation
```

A few properties of the output shown in Figure 3-1 are very important for provisioning virtual machines:

- `AvailableServices`
- `Name`

You can create a virtual machine only in locations where the `AvailableServices` list contains `PersistentVMRole`. The `AvailableServices` list can also contain a `HighMemory` value. This denotes locations where the A5, A6, A7, A8, A9, and future high-memory virtual machine configurations are available to be provisioned. The `Name` property is the value you will use to specify the location during the creation of resources.

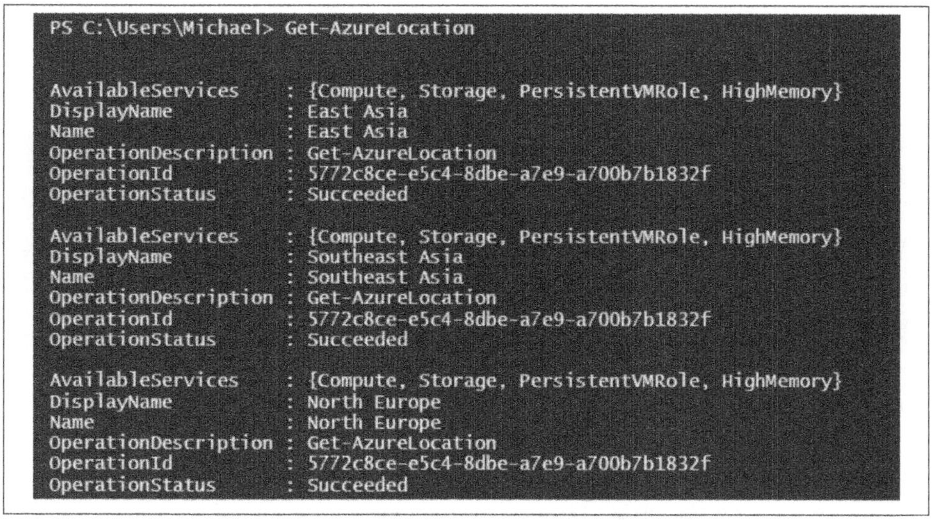

```
PS C:\Users\Michael> Get-AzureLocation

AvailableServices    : {Compute, Storage, PersistentVMRole, HighMemory}
DisplayName          : East Asia
Name                 : East Asia
OperationDescription : Get-AzureLocation
OperationId          : 5772c8ce-e5c4-8dbe-a7e9-a700b7b1832f
OperationStatus      : Succeeded

AvailableServices    : {Compute, Storage, PersistentVMRole, HighMemory}
DisplayName          : Southeast Asia
Name                 : Southeast Asia
OperationDescription : Get-AzureLocation
OperationId          : 5772c8ce-e5c4-8dbe-a7e9-a700b7b1832f
OperationStatus      : Succeeded

AvailableServices    : {Compute, Storage, PersistentVMRole, HighMemory}
DisplayName          : North Europe
Name                 : North Europe
OperationDescription : Get-AzureLocation
OperationId          : 5772c8ce-e5c4-8dbe-a7e9-a700b7b1832f
OperationStatus      : Succeeded
```

Figure 3-1. Using Get-AzureLocation

After you have determined the region in which to create virtual machines, you can store the name of the region in a variable for later reference. Add the code in Example 3-3 to your script to store the region name.

Example 3-3. Storing the region name in a variable (Script pane)

```
$location = "[region name]"
```

The next step is to specify the storage account where the virtual machines will be created. The storage account must be in the same region as the virtual machine. This is enforced at the API level so you do not accidentally end up in a situation where your virtual machine is running on the West Coast of the United States but the underlying disks are in Europe!

The first option is to enumerate your existing storage accounts for a suitable storage account. The command in Example 3-4 will enumerate all of the storage accounts in your subscription but return only the StorageAccountName and Location properties (see Figure 3-2).

Example 3-4. Enumerating existing storage accounts (Console pane)

```
Get-AzureStorageAccount | select StorageAccountName, Location
```

If you do not have a storage account available, or you just want to create a new one, use the New-AzureStorageAccount cmdlet.

To ensure the availability of the Microsoft Azure storage account name, you should use the Test-AzureName cmdlet first (see Example 3-5). Test-AzureName verifies whether the name is available for your use in Microsoft Azure. Make sure you replace the *[stor age account name]* placeholder in the script before executing!

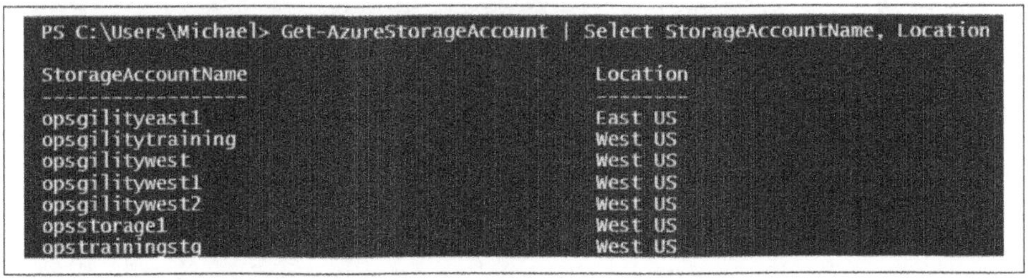

```
PS C:\Users\Michael> Get-AzureStorageAccount | Select StorageAccountName, Location

StorageAccountName                                    Location

opsgilityeast1                                        East US
opsgilitytraining                                     West US
opsgilitywest                                         West US
opsgilitywest1                                        West US
opsgilitywest2                                        West US
opsstorage1                                           West US
opstrainingstg                                        West US
```

Figure 3-2. Using Get-AzureStorageAccount to enumerate storage accounts

Example 3-5. Finding a unique storage account name (Console pane)

```
Test-AzureName -Storage -Name "[storage account name]"
```

If the call returns True, the storage account name already exists and is not available to you. Run the command with a new name until the call returns False, which means that the storage account name is available. Create the new storage account as shown in Example 3-6.

Storage account name

The name of your storage account must be unique within Azure. Storage account names must be between 3 and 24 characters in length and use numbers and lowercase letters only.

Example 3-6. Creating a new storage account (Console pane)

```
New-AzureStorageAccount -StorageAccountName "[storage account name]" `
                        -Location $location
```

When you determine the name of the storage account to use, save it in a variable for later reference. Add the code in Example 3-7 to your script to store the storage account name.

Example 3-7. Specifying the current storage account (Script pane)

```
$storageAccount = "[storage account name]"
```

The next step is to associate the storage account with the subscription you are using by specifying the name with the -CurrentStorageAccountName parameter in the Set-AzureSubscription cmdlet. Once set, any PowerShell cmdlets that create virtual machines or deploy cloud-service packages will use this storage account as the default.

Add the code in Example 3-8 to associate the subscription with the storage account.

Example 3-8. Specifying the current storage account (Script pane)

```
Set-AzureSubscription -SubscriptionName $subscription `
                      -CurrentStorageAccountName $storageAccount
```

Selecting the Virtual Machine Platform Image

When creating a virtual machine, you can start from an existing disk or from one of the platform images in Microsoft Azure. In Chapter 5 I will cover provisioning virtual machines directly from disk. For now, this chapter will focus on using an image. To view the available images for your subscription run the command `Get-AzureVMImage`, as shown in Example 3-9.

Example 3-9. Enumerating virtual machine images (Console pane)

```
Get-AzureVMImage
```

The amount of information that `Get-AzureVMImage` returns can be quite overwhelming (see Figure 3-3).

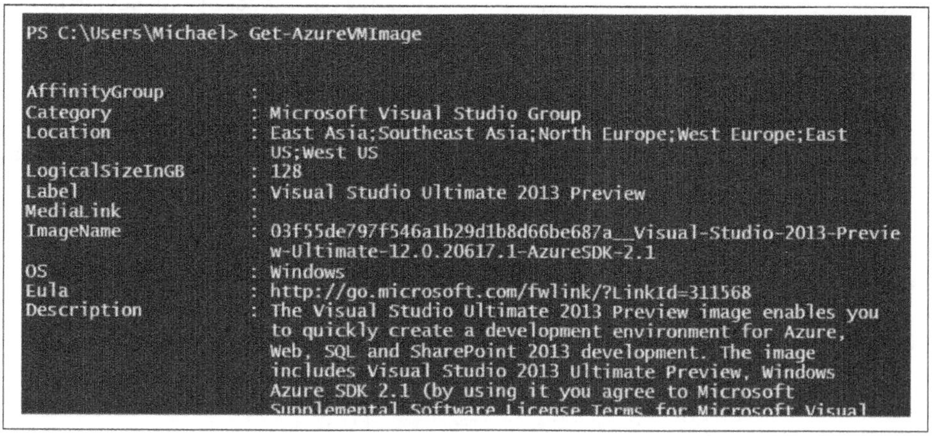

Figure 3-3. Output from Get-AzureVMImage

Table 3-1 lists some important properties to note.

Table 3-1. Get-AzureVMImage properties

EULA	This is a link to an end-user license agreement for the particular image.
LogicalDiskSizeInGB	Shows how large the OS disk will be if you use this image (maximum 127 GB).
RecommendedVMSize	The recommended size to run this image.
IsPremium	If True, you are paying above standard compute rates for the operating system. SQL Server is a good example, as you are paying a premium for the SQL Server licensing cost.

Description	Description of what the image contains.
ImageFamily	A name to group the same type of images. There are multiple images of the same family due to creating new patched images and sometimes configuration differences.
ImageName	When provisioning from PowerShell, this is the value you will use when specifying the image.

Thankfully, PowerShell provides the ability to quickly filter out information.

The first step is to identify the image family by using the Get-AzureVMImage cmdlet and returning only the ImageFamily property (see Example 3-10).

Example 3-10. Returning all available image families (Console pane)

```
Get-AzureVMImage | select ImageFamily
```

When you have identified the image family that you want to use, assign the image family name to a variable. You can use that variable with PowerShell's native comparison and filter capabilities to always return the latest image for that family and store that image name in a variable for later use.

The code in Example 3-11 returns a list of available images, and then passes that output to the where command, which filters only images with the image family name that matches $imageFamily. That output is then sorted by PublishedDate (Descending) so the newest image is the first one returned. Finally, that output is then passed to the select command with the -First parameter, which indicates to return only the first item.

Add the code in Example 3-11 to your script to return and store the name of the virtual machine image to use.

Example 3-11. Finding the latest image name (Script pane)

```
$imageFamily = "Windows Server 2012 R2 Datacenter"

$imageName = Get-AzureVMImage |
             where { $_.ImageFamily -eq $imageFamily } |
             sort PublishedDate -Descending |
             select -ExpandProperty ImageName -First 1
```

Virtual Machine Size

The Get-AzureRoleSize cmdlet can be used to enumerate the available virtual machine sizes (see Example 3-12). This will tell you the maximum memory, the maximum size on the resource disk, and the number of data disks supported per role (see Figure 3-4).

Example 3-12. Identifying the virtual machine size (Console pane)

```
Get-AzureRoleSize
```

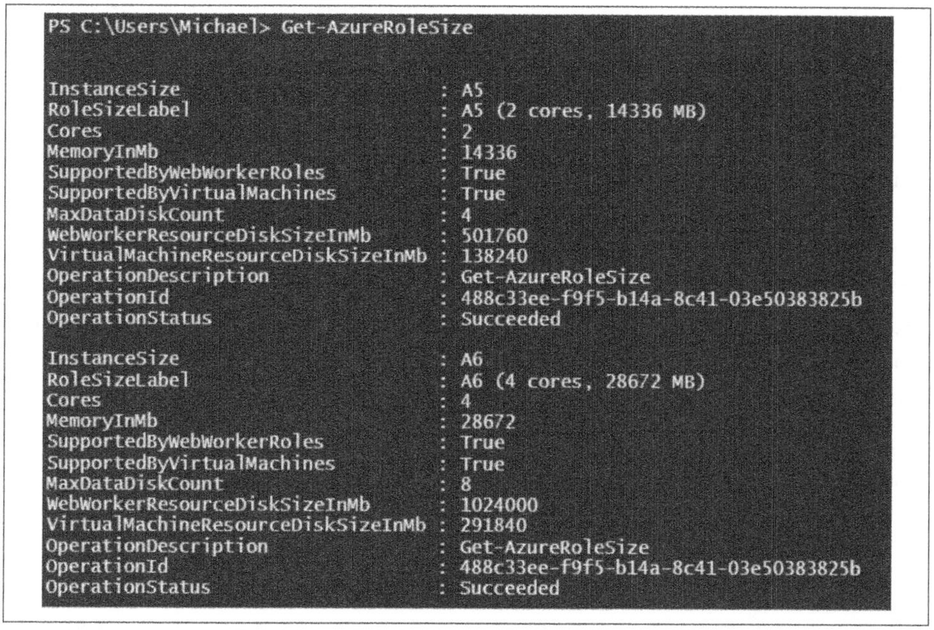

```
PS C:\Users\Michael> Get-AzureRoleSize

InstanceSize                      : A5
RoleSizeLabel                     : A5 (2 cores, 14336 MB)
Cores                             : 2
MemoryInMb                        : 14336
SupportedByWebWorkerRoles         : True
SupportedByVirtualMachines        : True
MaxDataDiskCount                  : 4
WebWorkerResourceDiskSizeInMb     : 501760
VirtualMachineResourceDiskSizeInMb : 138240
OperationDescription              : Get-AzureRoleSize
OperationId                       : 488c33ee-f9f5-b14a-8c41-03e50383825b
OperationStatus                   : Succeeded

InstanceSize                      : A6
RoleSizeLabel                     : A6 (4 cores, 28672 MB)
Cores                             : 4
MemoryInMb                        : 28672
SupportedByWebWorkerRoles         : True
SupportedByVirtualMachines        : True
MaxDataDiskCount                  : 8
WebWorkerResourceDiskSizeInMb     : 1024000
VirtualMachineResourceDiskSizeInMb : 291840
OperationDescription              : Get-AzureRoleSize
OperationId                       : 488c33ee-f9f5-b14a-8c41-03e50383825b
OperationStatus                   : Succeeded
```

Figure 3-4. Using Get-AzureRoleSize

Ensure that the size you select has `SupportedByVirtualMachines` set to `True`. Since this is PowerShell, you can filter output on that property (see Example 3-13).

Example 3-13. Returning only role sizes supported by virtual machines (Console pane)

```
Get-AzureRoleSize | where { $_.SupportedByVirtualMachines -eq $true }
```

When you have identified which role size to use to create your virtual machines, simply store the `InstanceSize` name in a variable.

Add the code in Example 3-14 to store the virtual machine size.

Example 3-14. Storing the virtual machine size (Script pane)

```
$vmSize = "Small"
```

Cloud Services and Virtual Machines

are always created in a container called a *cloud service*. A cloud service provides a networking and security boundary for your virtual machines. Virtual machines that are created in the same cloud service are on the same private network and can directly communicate with each other without going through the public load balancer or a virtual network to communicate.

Also, if virtual machines need to be load-balanced together or require high availability, they must be created in the same cloud service as load-balanced endpoints (internal and external), and availability sets cannot span multiple cloud services. Microsoft Azure also provides built-in name resolution to virtual machines in the same cloud service.

During virtual machine creation, you are required either to specify the cloud service name for an existing cloud service that is available in your subscription or to supply a new name that is not in use and is globally available. In this chapter you will use PowerShell to create a new cloud service.

Just like the name of a Microsoft Azure storage account, a cloud service name must be globally unique in Microsoft Azure. To ensure the availability of the cloud service name, use the Test-AzureName cmdlet first (see Example 3-15).

Ensure that you replace the *[cloud service name]* placeholder with the name of the cloud service you wish to create.

Example 3-15. Finding a unique cloud service name (Console pane)

```
Test-AzureName -Service -Name "[cloud service name]"
```

If the call returns True, the service name exists and cannot be created again (this does not indicate whether the service is in your subscription). In this example, we specifically want to create a new cloud service, so you should run the command with a new name until the call returns False. When you have identified a unique name, store it in a variable for later reference.

Add the code in Example 3-16 to your script to store the cloud service name.

Example 3-16. Store the cloud service name in a variable (Script pane)

```
$serviceName = "[cloud service name]"
```

Creating a Virtual Machine with New-AzureQuickVM

The New-AzureQuickVM cmdlet is very similar to using the Quick Create button in the Microsoft Azure management portal. The available customizations are limited, but it is a relatively easy way of provisioning a virtual machine.

To use this technique, you will need to define three more variables: the administrator username, the password, and the computer name. When choosing the name and password for the local administrator account, ensure that the values you choose are not overly obvious, like "administrator" or "password", because the Microsoft Azure API will reject them. Add the code in Example 3-17 to your script and replace the placeholder values with values of your own.

Example 3-17. Username, password, and computer name (Script pane)

```
# Specify the admin credentials
$adminUser = "[admin username]"
$password = "[admin password]"

# Specify the virtual machine name
$vmName = "ps-vm1"
```

Storing usernames and passwords in scripts

As a general rule, it is a bad security practice and a bad mainte-
nance practice to store credentials directly in a script. It is shown
here to keep the scripts simple and focus on the task at hand. Practical alternatives include passing credentials in as parameters to a
script or prompting for credentials by using the Get-Credential
cmdlet.

Computer name uniqueness

The computer name must be unique to all of the virtual machines in
the same cloud service.

Now that all of the necessary information is stored in variables, you can create a virtual
machine (VM).

The New-AzureQuickVM cmdlet supports parameter sets for creating Windows- or
Linux-based virtual machines from an image. In this example, passing -Windows tells
the cmdlets that the image you are passing is a Windows-based OS.

Add the code in Example 3-18 to your script.

Example 3-18. Creating a virtual machine using New-AzureQuickVM (Script pane)

```
New-AzureQuickVM -Windows `
                 -ServiceName $serviceName `
                 -Name $vmName `
                 -ImageName $imageName `
                 -Location $location `
                 -InstanceSize $vmSize `
                 -AdminUsername $adminUser `
                 -Password $password
```

This technique is quick and simple but it does have its drawbacks. The limitations to
using New-AzureQuickVM are as follows:

- You cannot add data disks or endpoints at creation time.
- You cannot have the virtual machine domain-joined at creation time.

- You cannot boot from a disk (images only).

Several other provisioning features supported by New-AzureQuickVM are discussed in Chapter 7.

Creating a Virtual Machine Configuration with New-AzureVMConfig

The second technique for creating a virtual machine requires the use of two (or more) cmdlets together to compose a virtual machine by creating a configuration object, modifying it, and then creating a virtual machine with the customized configuration object. This pattern is similar to how the cmdlets are used for updating existing virtual machines.

As the name New-AzureVMConfig implies, this cmdlet does not create a virtual machine but instead creates a virtual machine configuration object. Once it is created, you modify the configuration object with other cmdlets to have all of the characteristics that you want the virtual machine to have at provisioning time. This technique can save you several API calls, such as individually adding data disks or network endpoints. If you are automating the creation of several virtual machines, this can save you a lot of time spent in provisioning and, in the long run, a lot of code you do not have to write.

Add the code in Example 3-19 to your script. Note that the $vmName variable has also been modified because this code will create a second virtual machine named ps-vm2 in the same cloud service as ps-vm1.

Example 3-19. Creating a VM configuration object with New-AzureVMConfig (Script pane)

```
$vmName = "ps-vm2"

$vmConfig = New-AzureVMConfig -Name $vmName `
                        -InstanceSize $vmSize `
                        -ImageName $imageName
```

When the virtual machine configuration is created, you then modify it using the PowerShell pipeline and several other Microsoft Azure cmdlets that know how to modify this object.

Specifying the Initial Provisioning Configuration

Creating a virtual machine configuration from an image, as shown in the previous example, requires you to specify the initial provisioning configuration. Use the Add-AzureProvisioningConfig cmdlet to specify these settings (see Example 3-20). This cmdlet accepts the passed-in object $vmConfig and modifies it by creating and setting the properties that will hold the local administrator username, password, and various other properties that can be set at provisioning time.

Example 3-20. Specifying the provisioning configuration (Script pane)

```
$vmConfig | Add-AzureProvisioningConfig -Windows `
                                        -AdminUsername $adminUser `
                                        -Password $password
```

Adding Storage with Add-AzureDataDisk

Creating virtual machines by composing the configuration allows you to specify additional information such as adding data disks at provisoning time. The amount of storage you can specify per virtual machine depends on the instance size you are creating. Each disk can be up to 1023 GB in size. Each virtual machine size allows a different number of data disks to be attached. The output from the `Get-AzureRoleSize` cmdlet used earlier will show the maximum number of data disks supported.

In Example 3-21 `Add-AzureDataDisk` with the `-CreateNew` parameter is used to modify the passed-in configuration `$vmConfig` to create blank, unformatted VHDs attached to the virtual machine on boot.

Add the code in Example 3-21 to your script to attach a new 500 GB data disk on LUN 0 of the virtual machine that will be created.

Example 3-21. Adding storage at provisioning time (Script pane)

```
$vmConfig | Add-AzureDataDisk -CreateNew `
                              -DiskSizeInGB 500 `
                              -DiskLabel "data 1" `
                              -LUN 0
```

> **Maximum data disk size**
>
> The maximum size of a data disk in Microsoft Azure is currently 1023 GB.

The `Add-AzureDataDisk` cmdlet supports three parameter sets. As shown in Example 3-21, the `-CreateNew` parameter is used to create blank VHDs. The `-Import` parameter allows you to specify a disk by referencing the name of the disk registered in Microsoft Azure. The `-ImportFrom` parameter allows you to specify the URL to the VHD in a Microsoft Azure storage account (in the same subscription and same region) and a disk label.

I will cover managing disks, images, and storage in greater detail in Chapter 5.

Creating Network Endpoints at Provisioning

Similar to adding storage, you can also add network endpoints at provisioning time by modifying the virtual machine configuration before passing it to Microsoft Azure for creation.

Example 3-22 modifies the virtual machine configuration $vmConfig by adding a new load-balanced endpoint named HTTP to the configuration.

This endpoint is using TCP as the protocol accepting traffic on public port 80 and forwarding it to local port 80. The -LBSetName parameter specifies that this endpoint is part of a load-balanced set. If I wanted to create additional virtual machines to handle additional traffic on port 80, I would just need to reference the same load-balanced set name as specified in the following example.

The -DefaultProbe parameter tells Microsoft Azure to set up a TCP health probe on the local port. This means that the load balancer will occasionally attempt to connect on the port specified with -LocalPort. If it can connect, the endpoint is considered healthy, but if it cannot connect after a configurable number of tries, then it will no longer be considered healthy and the load balancer will not forward traffic to the endpoint.

Add the code in Example 3-22 to modify your $vmConfig to add the load-balanced endpoint.

Example 3-22. Adding a load-balanced endpoint (Script pane)

```
$vmConfig | Add-AzureEndpoint -Name "HTTP" `
                              -Protocol tcp `
                              -LocalPort 80 `
                              -PublicPort 80 `
                              -LBSetName "LBHTTP" `
                              -DefaultProbe
```

As with data disks, I can add more endpoints if needed just by adding another call to Add-AzureEndpoint. In Example 3-22 I have added an endpoint for port 80 for HTTP traffic. I could also open up port 443 for HTTPS traffic simply by adding an endpoint to the configuration (see Example 3-23).

Example 3-23. Opening up port 443 (Script pane)

```
$vmConfig | Add-AzureEndpoint -Name "HTTPS" `
                              -Protocol tcp `
                              -LocalPort 443 `
                              -PublicPort 443 `
                              -LBSetName "LBHTTPS" `
                              -DefaultProbe
```

I will cover managing endpoints in greater detail in Chapter 4.

Creating a Virtual Machine with New-AzureVM

The cmdlet that does the heavy lifting of actually creating virtual machines from one or more configuration objects is New-AzureVM. The New-AzureVM cmdlet supports passing a single configuration object or an array of configuration objects to the -VMs parameter (see Example 3-24). If passed an array, the cmdlet will automatically create each virtual machine in the same cloud service for you.

Example 3-24. Creating a virtual machine with New-AzureVM (Script pane)

```
New-AzureVM -ServiceName $serviceName -VMs $vmConfig
```

Now that the last line of code is added, let me add a complete example (see Example 3-25) using placeholder values (ensure that you replace them with real values), and then I will review what the script does.

Example 3-25. Complete script for chapter3create.ps1 (Script pane)

```
# Replace with your own subscription name
$subscription = "[subscription name]"

Select-AzureSubscription $subscription

# Replace with the region you wish to deploy in
$location = "[region name]"

$vmSize = "Small"

# Replace with your own storage account name
$storageAccount = "[storage account name]"

Set-AzureSubscription -SubscriptionName $subscription `
                      -CurrentStorageAccountName $storageAccount

$imageFamily = "Windows Server 2012 R2 Datacenter"

$imageName = Get-AzureVMImage |
             where { $_.ImageFamily -eq $imageFamily } |
             sort PublishedDate -Descending |
             select -ExpandProperty ImageName -First 1

# Replace with a unique cloud service name
$serviceName = "[cloud service name]"

# Specify the admin credentials
$adminUser = "[admin user name]"
$password = "[admin password]"

# Specify the computer name
$vmName = "ps-vm1"
```

```
New-AzureQuickVM -Windows `
                 -ServiceName $serviceName `
                 -Name $vmName `
                 -ImageName $imageName `
                 -Location $location `
                 -InstanceSize $vmSize `
                 -AdminUsername $adminUser `
                 -Password $password


$vmName = "ps-vm2"

$vmConfig = New-AzureVMConfig -Name $vmName `
                              -InstanceSize $vmSize `
                              -ImageName $imageName

$vmConfig | Add-AzureProvisioningConfig -Windows `
                                        -AdminUsername $adminUser `
                                        -Password $password

$vmConfig | Add-AzureDataDisk -CreateNew `
                              -DiskSizeInGB 500 `
                              -DiskLabel "data 1" `
                              -LUN 0

$vmConfig | Add-AzureEndpoint -Name "HTTP" `
                              -Protocol tcp `
                              -LocalPort 80 `
                              -PublicPort 80 `
                              -LBSetName "LBHTTP" `
                              -DefaultProbe

$vmConfig | Add-AzureEndpoint -Name "HTTPS" `
                              -Protocol tcp `
                              -LocalPort 443 `
                              -PublicPort 443 `
                              -LBSetName "LBHTTPS" `
                              -DefaultProbe

New-AzureVM -ServiceName $serviceName -VMs $vmConfig
```

This script performs the following operations:

1. The script selects your subscription so that any Microsoft Azure cmdlet that is executed afterward runs against the correct subscription.

2. The script then updates your subscription to specify the `CurrentStorageAccount Name` property, which is really just a shortcut so you do not have to specify the storage account to use with each call.

3. The script returns the name of the latest image for the Server 2012 R2 Datacenter image family. This image name is required to tell the Microsoft Azure PowerShell cmdlets which image to use.

4. The script creates a new virtual machine named ps-vm1 by using the New-AzureQuickVM cmdlet. This cmdlet also creates the cloud service container for the virtual machine.

5. The script creates a new virtual machine configuration for a virtual machine named ps-vm2. This configuration has one data disk added and two network endpoints (HTTP and HTTPS).

6. The New-AzureVM cmdlet actually creates the ps-vm2 virtual machine and, by omitting the -Location parameter, creates the virtual machine in the same cloud service as ps-vm1.

Now that you understand what the script is intended to do, simply press F5, or highlight the script and press F8 to execute.

How New-AzureVM Works

The New-AzureVM cmdlet accepts a cloud service name, an array of configuration objects, a location or affinity group, and optionally a virtual network name. Provisioning virtual machines inside a virtual network will be discussed later.

Under the covers, New-AzureVM performs several activities against the Microsoft Azure Service Management API on your behalf. If you specify the -Location or -AffinityGroup parameter, the cmdlet will first create the cloud service container in the location or affinity group you specify. The cmdlet will then loop through the array of virtual machine configuration objects passed to it and create the virtual machines in the cloud service. The New-AzureVM cmdlet performs the serialization required to create multiple virtual machines if passed more than one configuration object. Serialization is required because virtual machines created in the same cloud service or the same virtual network must be created one by one due to locks put in place at the API level.

The New-AzureVM behavior regarding creating a new cloud service or using an existing cloud service depends on the -Location or -AffinityGroup parameters passed to it. If you want the cmdlet to create a new cloud service, simply specify one of the location parameters (-Location or -AffinityGroup). Passing either of these parameters tells the cmdlet that you want to create a new cloud service in the specified location or affinity group.

To create a virtual machine in an existing cloud service, simply omit the parameters (-Location or -AffinityGroup), and New-AzureVM will assume that the cloud service exists in your subscription and will attempt to create the virtual machine in that cloud service. In the previous code example, `-Location` was omitted because the cloud service was created with the previous call to `New-AzureQuickVM`.

Cloud service conflicts with New-AzureVM

When you run `New-AzureVM`, you might see: "WARNING: The specified DNS name is already taken." This means that the `-ServiceName` you have specified already exists. If the cloud service is part of your subscription and in the same region of the virtual machine you are going to create, you can ignore the warning or simply omit `-Location` or `-AffinityGroup` to avoid it altogether. If the cloud service name is owned by another Microsoft Azure subscription, the warning will be followed by an error: "New-AzureVM: ResourceNot-Found: The hosted service does not exist." This is beyond your control, and it is time to pick a new name for your cloud service!

Querying Virtual Machines with Get-AzureVM

The `Get-AzureVM` cmdlet is very useful for managing virtual machines. It has three distinct behaviors that allow you to perform some fairly advanced operations.

Run `Get-AzureVM` without passing any parameters, and the cmdlet will enumerate all of the virtual machines in your subscription (see Example 3-26 and Figure 3-5). Depending on how many virtual machines you have, this can be a lengthy operation. The architecture of the Microsoft Azure API requires that the cmdlet query the available virtual machines per cloud service. So if you have 100 cloud services, each with 1 virtual machine, the cmdlet will have to make 100 round-trips to the Microsoft Azure Service Management API.

Example 3-26. Viewing the status of your virtual machines (Console pane)

```
Get-AzureVM
```

The `Get-AzureVM` cmdlet can also return the detailed configuration of one or more virtual machines.

To return detailed configuration, you must specify the cloud service name and optionally the name of the virtual machine (see Example 3-27 and Figure 3-6). If the name of the virtual machine is specified with the `-Name` parameter, the `Get-AzureVM` cmdlet will return the configuration for only that virtual machine. If a virtual machine name is not specified, `Get-AzureVM` returns the configuration for all of the virtual machines in the cloud service.

Example 3-27. Returning virtual machine configuration (Console pane)

```
Get-AzureVM -ServiceName $serviceName
```

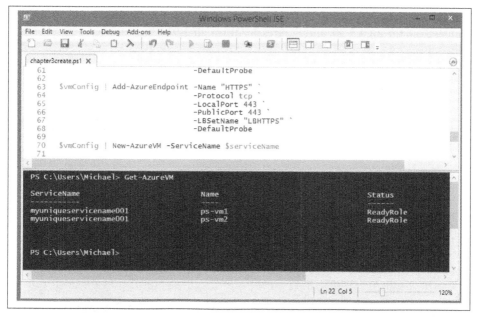

Figure 3-5. Querying virtual machine status with Get-AzureVM

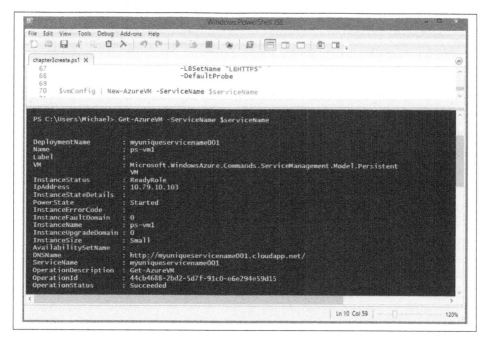

Figure 3-6. Querying virtual machine configuration with Get-AzureVM

The detailed configuration can be inspected using standard PowerShell operators or by using helper cmdlets that are part of the Microsoft Azure PowerShell cmdlets (see Examples 3-28 through 3-30, and Figures 3-7 through 3-9).

Example 3-28. Viewing endpoint configuration (Script console)

```
Get-AzureVM -ServiceName $serviceName | Get-AzureEndpoint
```

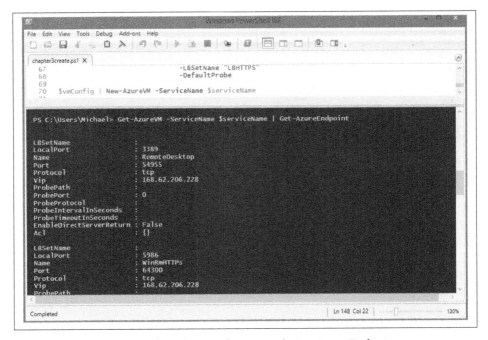

Figure 3-7. Viewing virtual machine endpoints with Get-AzureEndpoint

Example 3-29. Viewing data disk configuration

```
Get-AzureVM -ServiceName $serviceName | Get-AzureDataDisk
```

Example 3-30. Viewing OS disk configuration (Console pane)

```
Get-AzureVM -ServiceName $serviceName | Get-AzureOSDisk
```

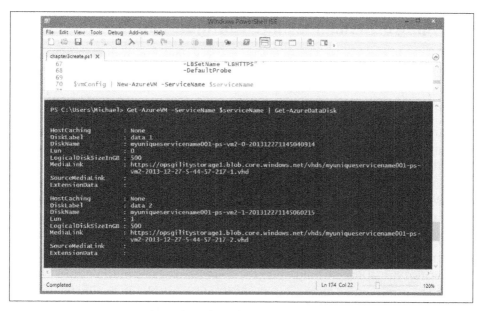

Figure 3-8. Viewing virtual machine data disk configuration with Get-AzureDataDisk

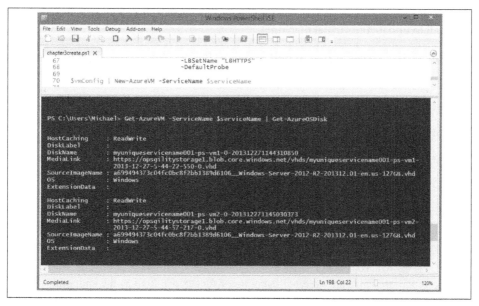

Figure 3-9. Viewing a virtual machine OS disk configuration with Get-AzureOSDisk

Changing a Virtual Machine Configuration

Updating a Microsoft Azure virtual machine is very similar to creating a new one. The difference is that instead of creating a new virtual machine configuration object, you are retrieving an existing configuration from the virtual machine that you want to update.

To retrieve an existing virtual machine configuration, use the `Get-AzureVM` cmdlet, passing the name of the cloud service and optionally the name of the virtual machine. Once the configuration is retrieved, you then modify it with the changes you want, using the same cmdlets used during creation. To make the final changes, call the `Update-AzureVM` cmdlet instead of `New-AzureVM`. `Update-AzureVM` accepts the cloud service name and the virtual machine name and passes the configuration back to the Microsoft Azure Management API to perform the update.

Using the pattern of Get-Modify-Update, Example 3-31 retrieves the configuration of the specified virtual machine, indicating the cloud service name and the virtual machine name. The configuration is stored in the `$vmConfig` variable. To modify the configuration, the `$vmConfig` variable is piped to the `Remove-AzureEndpoint` cmdlet, which looks in the configuration for an endpoint named RemoteDesktop and removes it if it exists. When the `Remove-AzureEndpoint` cmdlet has removed the endpoint from the virtual machine configuration, it is then piped to `Update-AzureVM`, which makes the API call to update the virtual machine.

Example 3-31. Removing an endpoint from a virtual machine (Console pane)

```
$serviceName = "[cloud service name]"

$vmName = "ps-vm1"

$vmConfig = Get-AzureVM -ServiceName $serviceName -Name $vmName

$vmConfig | Remove-AzureEndpoint -Name "RemoteDesktop"

$vmConfig | Update-AzureVM
```

Remote desktop endpoint names

If you try the previous example against the ps-vm2 virtual machine, the code will not work. Virtual machines created with the New-AzureQuickVM cmdlet name the endpoint RemoteDesktop, and virtual machines created using New-AzureVM use RDP as the endpoint name. In Chapter 4 I will show how to identify endpoints by using the local port instead of the name.

The previous example removes the remote desktop endpoint from the specified virtual machine. Since the endpoint is removed, you can no longer use remote desktop to

---

connect to the virtual machine. You can try this on your own by executing the Get-AzureRemoteDesktopFile cmdlet to attempt a connection (see Example 3-32.

Example 3-32. Connecting to a virtual machine using remote desktop (Console pane)

```
Get-AzureRemoteDesktopFile -ServiceName $serviceName -Name $vmName -Launch
```

This can be very useful from a security perspective, as it gives you the ability to open up remote desktop only when needed and remove it when it is not. Later, I will show how to configure an access control list (ACL) to make this even more secure.

Now we will create another simple script that takes the ps-vm1 virtual machine and updates it to have the same network endpoints and data disk configuration that ps-vm2 was provisioned with, since it was created with New-AzureVMConfig. We will also add the RemoteDesktop endpoint back and validate that connectivity works.

Create a new PowerShell script with the name *chapter3update.ps1* and add the code in Example 3-33. Ensure that you replace the placeholder values with the actual values for your subscription.

Example 3-33. Updating a virtual machine configuration (Script pane)

```
Select-AzureSubscription "[subscription name]"

$serviceName = "[cloud service name]"

$vmName = "ps-vm1"

$vmConfig = Get-AzureVM -ServiceName $serviceName -Name $vmName

$vmConfig | Add-AzureEndpoint -Name "RemoteDesktop" `
                              -LocalPort 3389 `
                              -Protocol TCP

$vmConfig | Add-AzureDataDisk -CreateNew `
                              -DiskSizeInGB 500 `
                              -DiskLabel "data 1" `
                              -LUN 0

$vmConfig | Add-AzureEndpoint -Name "HTTP" `
                              -Protocol tcp `
                              -LocalPort 80 `
                              -PublicPort 80 `
                              -LBSetName "LBHTTP" `
                              -DefaultProbe

$vmConfig | Add-AzureEndpoint -Name "HTTPS" `
                              -Protocol tcp `
                              -LocalPort 443 `
                              -PublicPort 443 `
                              -LBSetName "LBHTTPS" `
```

```
                              -DefaultProbe
```

```
$vmConfig | Update-AzureVM
```

Press F5 to execute the script, or highlight the script and press F8.

When the script has finished executing, run the `Get-AzureRemoteDesktopFile` cmdlet again from the console to verify that you can now connect to the virtual machine (see Example 3-34).

Example 3-34. Validating remote desktop connectivity (Console pane)

```
Get-AzureRemoteDesktopFile -ServiceName $serviceName -Name $vmName -Launch
```

Stopping and Starting Virtual Machines

The final topic of this chapter is a very important one for your pocketbook: stopping and starting virtual machines.

When you stop a virtual machine in Microsoft Azure using PowerShell or the portal (not from within the virtual machine), you are no longer billed for the compute time used (just for the storage cost for the underlying disks). As part of this book, I will point back to virtual machines created in previous topics and chapters so we don't have to re-create them with each example. With this in mind, it is likely a good idea to learn how to not be charged for virtual machines when not in use.

Example 3-35 will shut down all of the virtual machines in the cloud service. One of the limitations of Microsoft Azure is that if you shut down the last virtual machine in a cloud service without assigning a reserved IP address to the virtual machine, you will lose the public IP address (VIP) of the cloud service. This is why running the following code will prompt you to ensure that you are aware of this fact.

Example 3-35. Stopping all virtual machines in a cloud service (Console pane)

```
Get-AzureVM -ServiceName $serviceName | Stop-AzureVM
```

There are three things you can do to avoid the prompt shown in Figure 3-10:

- Pass the `-Force` parameter. This tells the cmdlet to not prompt you.
- Specify a reserved IP address. This feature will be discussed in more detail in Chapter 4.
- Pass the `-StayProvisioned` parameter. This tells the cmdlet to not deprovision the virtual machine and to just shut it down. However, you will still be charged for compute time when you use this switch, so it is not a good solution for saving money.

Figure 3-10. Warning regarding deployment IP

In addition to Stop-AzureVM, there are also Start-AzureVM and Restart-AzureVM. All three cmdlets accept the same -ServiceName and -Name parameters that correspond to the cloud service container name and the virtual machine name. They all accept pipeline output, as shown in the previous example, so you can run them against multiple virtual machines, if needed.

Summary

In this chapter we explored the basics of using the Microsoft Azure PowerShell cmdlets to create and configure a virtual machine. We learned how to use the Get-AzureLocation cmdlet to identify the Microsoft Azure regions that are available for virtual machines, and also to create them using the high-memory configurations.

This chapter also introduced the idea of using the virtual machine configuration object not only to create a virtual machine, but also to update an existing one by modifying the configuration and posting it back to the Microsoft Azure API by using the cmdlets. You will see this Get-Modify-Update pattern used throughout this book, as it is the underlying convention of the Microsoft Azure API and the command-line tools that use it.

In the next chapter we will dig deeper into virtual machine configuration by investigating the network stack in thorough detail from PowerShell.

## CHAPTER 4

Virtual Machine Networking

Automating the Network

In Chapter 3 we got our feet wet with creating and updating virtual machines, and as part of that we briefly covered modifying network endpoints by adding and removing them through PowerShell. In this chapter we will dive deeper and learn how to manage more-advanced scenarios such as configuring the load balancer, TCP and HTTP health probes, reserved IP addresses, and of course network security using access control lists (ACLs). We will discuss deploying a virtual machine into a virtual network in Chapter 6.

Handling External Traffic

With Microsoft Azure Virtual Machines, you have a lot of control over how network traffic from the outside world is managed. This control manifests itself in an entity that you can manage through the management portal and is surfaced through the API and ultimately to tools such as PowerShell; that entity is the endpoint.

What exactly is an endpoint? An *endpoint* is an inbound rule associated with a virtual machine that allows you to tell Microsoft Azure what do with incoming traffic. You can set many properties of the endpoint for different behaviors.

Port Forwarding

Port forwarding is a simple but powerful concept. An endpoint listens on a public port and forwards traffic to an internal port. The internal and public ports can be the same or different.

For instance, your cloud service might contain two virtual machines, and each virtual machine is listening on port 3389 for remote desktop. How do you connect to each virtual machine independently, using the single IP address of the cloud service? The answer is to use port forwarding and listen on distinct public ports that are then mapped to each virtual machine's internal IP address on port 3389, as shown in Figure 4-1.

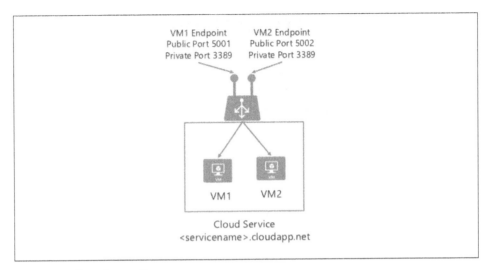

Figure 4-1. Port forwarding

This technique was demonstrated in Chapter 3 with the line of code shown in Example 4-1 that added the RemoteDesktop endpoint back to the virtual machine configuration.

Example 4-1. Adding a port-forwarded endpoint to a virtual machine

```
$vmConfig | Add-AzureEndpoint -Name "RemoteDesktop" `
                              -LocalPort 3389 `
                              -Protocol TCP
```

Since -LBSetName (load-balanced set name) is not specified, this indicates that traffic to the endpoint will apply to only the individual virtual machine to which it has been added and will not be load-balanced.

What is missing in the code from this discussion is the public port. When using the PowerShell cmdlets, if you do not specify the -PublicPort parameter, Microsoft Azure will automatically select an unused port on your behalf. You are still free to specify the -PublicPort parameter if you choose, as long as the public port does not conflict with any other endpoints in the same cloud service.

Load Balancing

Load balancing is fundamentally the same concept as port forwarding. You are still telling the endpoint to forward traffic from a public port to a private port inside the cloud service. The difference is the load-balanced set argument that tells Microsoft Azure that the private port can be a set of one or more virtual machines (see Figure 4-2).

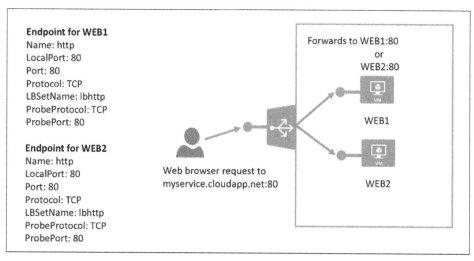

Figure 4-2. Load-balanced endpoints

Let's again review some of the code from the previous chapter (see Example 4-2).

Example 4-2. Adding a load-balanced endpoint

```
$vmConfig | Add-AzureEndpoint -Name "HTTP" `
                             -Protocol tcp `
                             -LocalPort 80 `
                             -PublicPort 80 `
                             -LBSetName "LBHTTP" `
                             -DefaultProbe
```

The difference between this endpoint being added and the RemoteDesktop endpoint are the -LBSetName and -DefaultProbe parameters. The -LBSetName parameter tells Microsoft Azure that other virtual machines within the same cloud service could also create an endpoint with the same public port, as long as they also share the same LBSetName without conflict.

If multiple virtual machines share an endpoint with the same public port and LBSet Name, Microsoft Azure will load-balance all traffic to the public port to each virtual machine in the set.

The -DefaultProbe parameter specifies that the PowerShell cmdlets should create a simple TCP health probe based on the private port.

> **Load-balancing algorithm**
>
> The Microsoft Azure load balancer for virtual machines currently
> supports only round-robin-style load balancing.

Health Probes

The Microsoft Azure load balancer supports health probes for load-balanced endpoints.
Health probes are features designed to give you more control and increase your application
availability.

You can configure health probes to monitor a TCP endpoint, or if you want more control, you can configure a probe against an HTTP endpoint.

TCP Health Probes

TCP-based endpoints are the simplest to configure. The Microsoft Azure load balancer
will attempt a connection on the internal IP and local port for the load-balanced endpoint.
If there is no acknowledgement (ACK) to the connection attempt after a configurable
time-out period, the load balancer will stop sending traffic to the virtual machine
on that endpoint. The health probe does continue to attempt a connection at a configurable
interval, and if the virtual machine starts responding to the probe, the load balancer
will start sending traffic to it again, as shown in Figure 4-3.

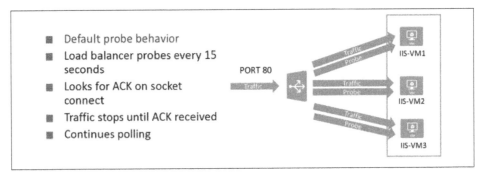

Figure 4-3. TCP health probe life cycle

The simplest method of enabling a TCP-based heath probe is to specify the
`-DefaultProbe` parameter on the load-balanced endpoint as it is being added. This will
automatically create a TCP-based health probe to which the load balancer attempts to
connect on the internal IP and local port.

The health probe can be configured on a separate port from the private port for the
endpoint. This allows you to have scenarios where a separate endpoint can be established

that just monitors health. For instance, there is no direct protocol support for UDP health probes. If you were to deploy a UDP service, you could also add a TCP-based endpoint to your service that responded for health probe requests.

In this example we will use our imagination and pretend we are configuring the load-balanced endpoint for a UDP-based service that listens on UDP port 5001.

I have modified the previous call to the Add-AzureEndpoint cmdlet to open a UDP-based endpoint that is listening on port 5001 locally and publicly. However, the load balancer will probe the new TCP-based endpoint that you added to your service on port 5051 to ensure that the service is healthy (see Example 4-3).

Example 4-3. Adding a load-balanced endpoint (UDP) with a custom TCP probe port

```
$vmConfig | Add-AzureEndpoint -Name "CUSTOMUDP" `
                             -Protocol udp `
                             -LocalPort 5001 `
                             -PublicPort 5001 `
                             -LBSetName "LBCUSTOMUDP" `
                             -ProbeProtocol tcp `
                             -ProbePort 5051
```

HTTP Health Probes

HTTP health endpoints allow you to have programmatic control over whether or not a virtual machine should be served traffic by the load balancer. How do you exert this control? Simply by writing a custom page (ASP, PHP, and so on) that performs whatever validation your application requires (database checks, writing to disk, and so on) and then returns an HTTP 200 for success or any other HTTP response for failure, as shown in Figure 4-4.

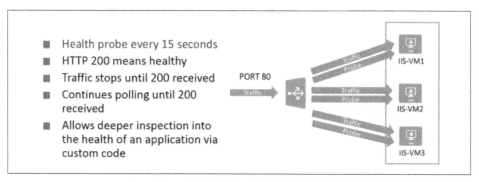

Figure 4-4. HTTP health probe life cycle

When the health probe code is written and deployed on the virtual machine, you simply tell the load-balanced endpoint configuration how to access it on the virtual machine, and Microsoft Azure will take care of the rest. The -ProbePort parameter allows you to have fine-grained control over how to access the probe (see Example 4-4).

Example 4-4. Adding a load-balanced endpoint with a custom HTTP probe

```
$vmConfig | Add-AzureEndpoint -Name "CUSTOMHTTP" `
                             -Protocol tcp `
                             -LocalPort 8080 `
                             -PublicPort 8080 `
                             -LBSetName "LBCUSTOMHTTP" `
                             -ProbeProtocol http `
                             -ProbePort 8080 `
                             -ProbePath '/healthcheck.aspx'
```

Troubleshooting

Since the load balancer is probing the probe endpoint, there is no way to specify authentication. This means you should ensure that the probe path will respond correctly to anonymous requests. Checking your web logs for the probe is a great way to determine if something is not working correctly.

Health Probe Time-outs

You can set two additional parameters when configuring TCP- or HTTP-based health probes, as shown in Table 4-1.

Table 4-1. Controlling the probe interval

-ProbeTimeIntervalInSeconds	Tells the load balancer how often to probe the endpoint. The minimum value you can set is 5 seconds, and the default value is 15 seconds.
-ProbeTimeoutInSeconds	Tells the load balancer how long to wait for a response before considering the probe a time-out. The minimum value is 11 seconds, with a default of 31 seconds.

Depending on the application, these default values may be fine. It is highly recommended to test health probe configurations with the application that they are monitoring to ensure that response times match expectations.

Example 4-5 shows a modified version of the previous example that demonstrates how the values can be set when creating the endpoint.

Example 4-5. Setting the probe interval and time-out values of a health probe

```
$vmConfig | Add-AzureEndpoint -Name "CUSTOMHTTP" `
                             -Protocol tcp `
                             -LocalPort 8080 `
                             -PublicPort 8080 `
                             -LBSetName "LBCUSTOMHTTP" `
                             -ProbeProtocol http `
                             -ProbePort 8080 `
```

```
-ProbePath '/healthcheck.aspx' `
-ProbeTimeIntervalInSeconds 30 `
-ProbeTimeoutInSeconds 62
```

Updating Endpoints

So far, all of the examples I have used have been focused on adding new endpoints either at virtual machine creation time or once the virtual machine has already been created. Another critical operation is updating an endpoint that already exists.

There are two cmdlets to help you with this task. The first is the `Set-AzureEndpoint` cmdlet. This cmdlet can be used to update an existing endpoint that is not part of a load-balanced set. This is an important distinction because, as you have seen in the last two sections, an endpoint can be created as a standalone or it can be created as part of a load-balanced set using the `Add-AzureEndpoint` cmdlet.

Updating an existing endpoint using `Set-AzureEndpoint` is a multistep operation, as this cmdlet simply modifies the virtual machine configuration and calls the Microsoft Azure API with the updated configuration.

Let's walk through several of the cmdlets needed to view and modify endpoint configuration. The first step is to return and store the virtual machine configuration as shown in Example 4-6.

Example 4-6. Returning the existing endpoint configuration (Console pane)

```
$serviceName = "[cloud service name]"

$vmName = "ps-vm1"

# Return the VM configuration (contains the endpoint configuration)
$vmConfig = Get-AzureVM -ServiceName $serviceName -Name $vmName
```

Piping the returned configuration to `Get-AzureEndpoint` allows you to see the endpoint configuration on the virtual machine. You can filter it to show only endpoints of interest as Example 4-7 does, or you can omit the endpoint name or any filters, and the cmdlet will show all of the endpoints on the virtual machine.

Example 4-7. Viewing the endpoint configuration filtering by port (Console pane)

```
$vmConfig | Get-AzureEndpoint | where LocalPort -eq 3389
```

To modify the endpoint, pipe the `$vmConfig` object to the `Set-AzureEndpoint` cmdlet and specify the existing endpoint name and the property you want to change. In this case, the code is changing the public port to 5099 (see Example 4-8).

Example 4-8. Modifying the endpoint configuration (Console pane)

```
$vmConfig | Set-AzureEndpoint "RemoteDesktop" -PublicPort 5099
```

The last step is to pipe the updated configuration to the `Update-AzureVM` cmdlet, as shown in Example 4-9.

Example 4-9. Updating the virtual machine (Console pane)

```
$vmConfig | Update-AzureVM
```

If you can use `Set-AzureEndpoint` for only a non-load-balanced endpoint, how do you modify the configuration of an endpoint in a load-balanced set? Great question! The answer is to use the `Set-AzureLoadBalancedEndpoint` cmdlet instead.

Why the need for a new cmdlet? As you can see from the previous example, `Set-AzureEndpoint` works on an entity tied to a specific virtual machine. Imagine that you have 50 virtual machines as part of a load-balanced set. To update one endpoint, you would be required to make 50 round-trips to the Microsoft Azure API. A more efficient approach was needed, and that approach was to introduce an API that allowed a single load-balanced endpoint to be updated, and that API is exposed by the `Set-AzureLoadBalancedEndpoint` cmdlet.

To demonstrate how to use this cmdlet, I will reuse the HTTP endpoint created earlier in this chapter.

Using the `Get-AzureEndpoint` cmdlet, I can review the existing properties of the endpoint (see Figure 4-5).

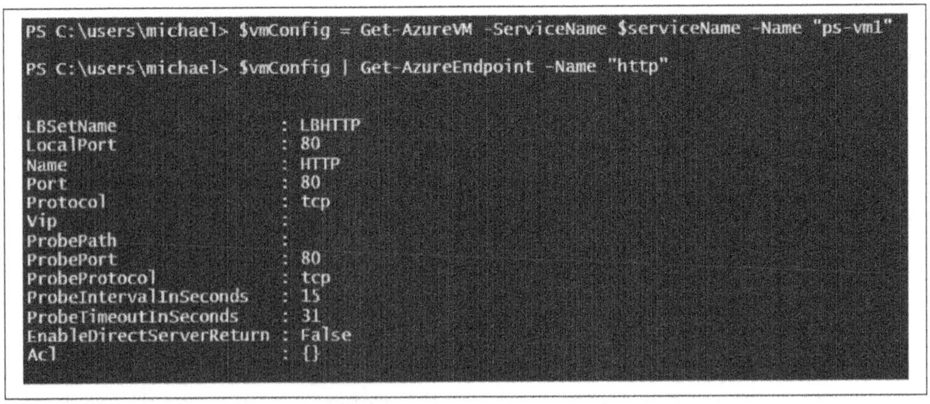

```
PS C:\users\michael> $vmConfig = Get-AzureVM -ServiceName $serviceName -Name "ps-vm1"

PS C:\users\michael> $vmConfig | Get-AzureEndpoint -Name "http"


LBSetName               : LBHTTP
LocalPort               : 80
Name                    : HTTP
Port                    : 80
Protocol                : tcp
Vip                     :
ProbePath               :
ProbePort               : 80
ProbeProtocol           : tcp
ProbeIntervalInSeconds  : 15
ProbeTimeoutInSeconds   : 31
EnableDirectServerReturn : False
Acl                     : {}
```

Figure 4-5. Using Get-AzureEndpoint

The `Set-AzureLoadBalancedEndpoint` cmdlet is much simpler, as it is working on a separate entity from the virtual machine configuration. It is a single command that requires only the cloud service name, the load-balanced set name, and of course whatever changes you wish to make to the endpoint.

Example 4-10 modifies the load-balanced endpoint set LBHTTP by changing it from the default probe (a basic TCP probe) to the more advanced HTTP probe.

Example 4-10. Updating a load-balanced endpoint (Console pane)

```
Set-AzureLoadBalancedEndpoint  -ServiceName $serviceName `
                               -ProbeProtocolHTTP `
                               -LBSetName "LBHTTP" `
                               -ProbePath "/healthcheck.aspx"
```

Access Control

Access control lists (ACLs) are configurable entities available to all virtual machine endpoints, whether they are load-balanced or not. An ACL is a list of rules that allows you to specify whether traffic from a specific network address space is permitted or not. Each ACL can have up to 50 rules, which allows for flexible configurations.

Creating an ACL is straightforward. You just need to call the `New-AzureAclConfig` cmdlet and store the resulting object in a variable (see Example 4-11).

Example 4-11. Creating an ACL object

```
$acl = New-AzureAclConfig
```

An ACL on its own is not very useful. To make it useful, the next step is to add rules. To add a rule, use the `Set-AzureAclConfig` cmdlet with the `-AddRule` parameter and specify the ACL you are modifying by using the `-ACL` parameter (see Example 4-12).

Each ACL rule has four properties that can be set, shown in Table 4-2.

Table 4-2. ACL rule properties

Order	ACL rules are processed by the Microsoft Azure packet filter in the order they are specified in the access control list.
RemoteSubnet	The remote subnet must be specified in CIDR format. This is the network to which the rule is applied.
Action	Can be either Permit or Deny. If a rule specifies that a specific RemoteSubnet is permitted, the packet filter will deny any other subnets; likewise, if a rule denies a subnet, other subnets are permitted (unless other rules block them).
Description	A field of text useful for adding a note for later reference on what the rule does.

Example 4-12. Adding a permit rule

```
Set-AzureAclConfig -AddRule -ACL $acl -Order 100 -Action Permit `
-RemoteSubnet "175.1.0.0/24" -Description "Allow Management Network"
```

After this rule is set, any IP that matches the 175.1.0.1/24 subnet will be allowed access (see Table 4-3). Since there are no other PERMIT rules in place, all other traffic will be denied access to the endpoint. You can add multiple rules to an ACL object and build up a much more complex rule table. For instance, to make the previous example accessible from multiple distinct remote subnets, just add a rule to the table when creating or updating the endpoint (see Example 4-13).

Table 4-3. ACL rule table

Order	Remote subnet	Endpoint	Permit/Deny
100	175.1.0.0/24	Remote Desktop	Permit

Example 4-13. Specifying an ACL with multiple rules

```
Set-AzureAclConfig -AddRule -ACL $acl -Order 100 -Action Permit `
-RemoteSubnet "175.1.0.0/24" -Description "Allow Management Network"

Set-AzureAclConfig -AddRule -ACL $acl -Order 200 -Action Permit `
-RemoteSubnet "137.135.67.39/32" -Description "Allow Management Server 1"
```

After these rules are added, clients from the 175.1.0.0/24 network or a client that matches the IP address of 137.135.67.39/32 are allowed access to the endpoint. All others will be rejected by the packet filter.

The new rule table would look like Table 4-4.

Table 4-4. New ACL rule table

Order	Remote subnet	Endpoint	Permit/Deny
100	175.1.0.0/24	Remote Desktop	Permit
200	137.135.67.39/32	Remote Desktop	Permit

The -Order parameter tells the packet filter the order in which to process the rules. The lower the order, the higher the priority.

Adding and Updating Access Control Lists

Now that you have seen how to create an ACL configuration object and modify it by adding rules to the ACL, the next step is to apply the ACL to an endpoint.

In this example I want to show a real-world use case: restricting access to the Remote-Desktop endpoint by using an ACL.

Example 4-14 declares a variable that contains the IP address that my Internet connection is using to the outside world. You can find this out on your own by browsing to Bing or Google and typing "What is my IP". The IP address is in CIDR format with the network address prefix of /32, which specifies a single IP address.

To try this on your own, create a new PowerShell script using the PowerShell ISE named *chapter4setacl.ps1*.

Example 4-14. Variables for applying an access control list to an endpoint (Script pane)

```
# Use the smallest range available (a single IP)
# Example: $myip = "12.153.189.234/32"

$myip = "[my ip address]/32"
$serviceName = "[cloud service name]"
$vmName = "ps-vm1"
```

The next step is to create the access control list configuration object and apply rules to it with the Set-AzureAclConfig cmdlet. Example 4-15 is specifying only a single permit rule that, once applied, allows only the remote subnet specified in the $myip variable access to the RemoteDesktop endpoint.

Example 4-15. Creating the access control list object (Script pane)

```
# Create the ACL configuration object
$acl = New-AzureAclConfig

# Add my IP address with permit
Set-AzureAclConfig -ACL $acl `
                   -AddRule Permit `
                   -RemoteSubnet $myip `
                   -Order 100 `
                   -Description "Allow RDP"
```

Since this example is adding an access control list to an existing endpoint, you first need to return the existing configuration of the virtual machine as it contains the existing configurations for all endpoints (see Example 4-16).

Example 4-16. Returning the existing endpoint configuration (Script pane)

```
# Return the VM configuration (contains the endpoint configuration)
$vmConfig = Get-AzureVM -ServiceName $serviceName `
                        -Name $vmName
```

The first line pipes the configuration object $vmConfig to the Set-AzureEndpoint cmdlet. This cmdlet modifies the endpoint configuration specified by the -Name parameter by adding the $acl object.

The endpoint configuration now has the ACL configuration associated with it. The next line updates the virtual machine configuration with the Update-AzureVM cmdlet (see Example 4-17).

Example 4-17. Applying the access control list to the endpoint (Script pane)

```
# Update the endpoint configuration by passing in the ACL
$vmConfig | Set-AzureEndpoint -Name "RemoteDesktop" -ACL $acl
```

```
# Update the VM
$vmConfig | Update-AzureVM
```

When you have specified your IP address and the correct cloud service name, you can execute the script by pressing F5, or by highlighting the script and pressing F8.

Example 4-18 shows the full source of the previous example.

Example 4-18. Full source of the example

```
# Use the smallest range available (a single IP)
# Example: $myip = "12.153.189.234/32"

$myip = "[my ip address]/32"
$serviceName = "[cloud service name]"
$vmName = "ps-vm1"

# Create the ACL configuration object
$acl = New-AzureAclConfig

# Add my IP address with permit
Set-AzureAclConfig -ACL $acl `
                   -AddRule Permit `
                   -RemoteSubnet $myip `
                   -Order 100 `
                   -Description "Allow RDP"


# Return the VM configuration
$vmConfig = Get-AzureVM -ServiceName $serviceName `
                        -Name $vmName

# Update the endpoint configuration by passing in the ACL
$vmConfig | Set-AzureEndpoint -Name "RemoteDesktop" -ACL $acl

# Update the VM
$vmConfig | Update-AzureVM
```

The previous example shows you how you can add an access control list to an existing endpoint. Specifying the access control list at endpoint creation is a simpler operation. All that is needed is to create and configure the ACL configuration object, and then pass it to the -ACL parameter of the Add-AzureEndpoint cmdlet.

Example 4-19 is a partial example that shows that scenario.

Example 4-19. Specifying an access control list on endpoint creation

```
$remoteip = "137.117.17.7/32"

# Create the ACL configuration object
$acl = New-AzureAclConfig
```

```
# Add IP address with permit
Set-AzureAclConfig -ACL $acl `
                   -AddRule Permit `
                   -RemoteSubnet $remoteip `
                   -Order 100 `
                   -Description "Allow Access"

$vmConfig | Add-AzureEndpoint -Name "SQLSERVER" `
                              -Protocol tcp `
                              -LocalPort 1433 `
                              -PublicPort 1433 `
                              -ACL $acl


### Create virtual machine code here ###
```

Reserved IP Addresses

Reserved IP addresses allow you to create a named public IP address that does not change. This IP address can be assigned to a cloud service at creation time.

If a cloud service is assigned a reserved IP address, you can safely deallocate all of the virtual machines within it and not worry about the external IP address changing. If you delete a cloud service and all of the virtual machines within it, you can reuse the reserved IP address by creating another cloud service, or delete it altogether.

Example 4-20 creates a new reserved IP address using the name "My Reserved IP". A reserved IP address is always created in a specific region, and only cloud services from within the same region can use it. Figure 4-6 shows example output from creating a reserved IP.

Example 4-20. Creating a new reserved IP address (Console pane)

```
$reservedIP = "My Reserved IP"
$location = "[region name]"

New-AzureReservedIP -ReservedIPName $reservedIP -Location $location
```

Figure 4-6. Creating a reserved IP address

To view reserved IP addresses in your subscription (see Figure 4-7), you can use the Get-AzureReservedIP cmdlet (see Example 4-21). If you do not specify the name of the reserved IP, the cmdlet will return all of them.

Example 4-21. Enumerating reserved IPs

```
Get-AzureReservedIP
```

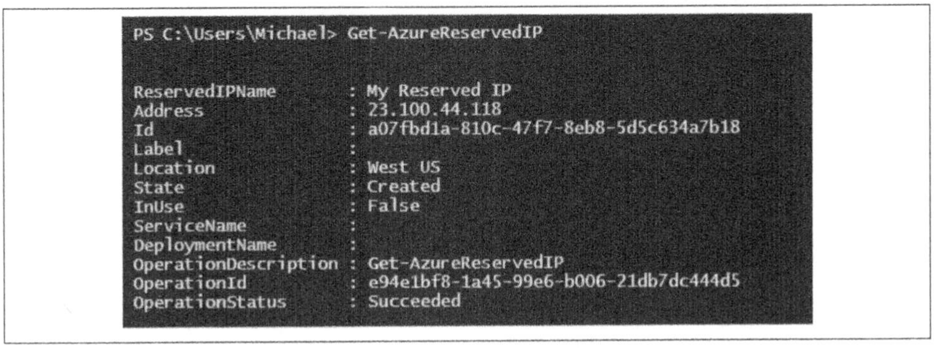

Figure 4-7. Viewing existing reserved IP addresses

When the reserved IP address has been created, you can then assign it to the cloud service container of your virtual machines at creation time.

To try this on your own, create a new PowerShell script named *chapter4reservedip.ps1* and add the code shown in Example 4-22. Ensure that you have created a reserved IP using the New-AzureReservedIP cmdlet and then replace the placeholder values with real values from your subscription.

Example 4-22. Creating a new virtual machine deployment with a reserved IP (Script pane)

```
$serviceName = "[cloud service name]"

# Specify the admin credentials
$adminUser = "[admin username]"
$password = "[admin password]"

# Specify the region to create the virtual machine in
# Must match the region of the reserved IP
$location = "[region name]"

# Specify your reserved IP name here
$reservedIP = "[the name of your reserved IP]"

# Specify the virtual machine name
$vmName = "ps-reservedip1"
```

```
$vmSize = "Small"

$imageFamily = "Windows Server 2012 R2 Datacenter"

$imageName = Get-AzureVMImage |
            where { $_.ImageFamily -eq $imageFamily } |
            sort PublishedDate -Descending |
            select -ExpandProperty ImageName -First 1

# Create a virtual machine configuration object
$vm1 = New-AzureVMConfig -Name $vmName -InstanceSize $vmSize -ImageName $imageName |
    Add-AzureProvisioningConfig -Windows `
                                -AdminUsername $adminUser `
                                -Password $password

# Specify the reserved IP address for the external VIP
New-AzureVM -ServiceName $serviceName -Location $location `
            -VMs $vm1 `
            -ReservedIPName $reservedIP
```

Reserved IPs set at creation

Reserved IP address settings are specified on the virtual machine deployment object. This object is created when the first virtual machine is created within a cloud service and cannot be updated after creation. If you would like to use a reserved IP address with your virtual machines, you must specify it at creation time. If you have existing virtual machines to use a reserved IP with, see Chapter 7, where I discuss importing and exporting virtual machines. This allows you to re-create the virtual machines with new deployment settings with the cost of some minor downtime.

Removing a reserved IP is simple as long as it is not in use. Simply run `Remove-AzureReservedIP` and specify the name of the IP to delete (see Example 4-23). When the IP is removed, it is gone forever and is not recoverable. There cannot be an existing deployment of virtual machines associated with the reserved IP address when running `Remove-AzureReservedIP`.

Example 4-23. Removing a reserved IP

```
Remove-AzureReservedIP -ReservedIPName "[the name of your reserved IP]"
```

Public IP Addresses

Public IP addresses are specific to a virtual machine instead of being specific to the cloud service, such as reserved IPs (see Figure 4-8).

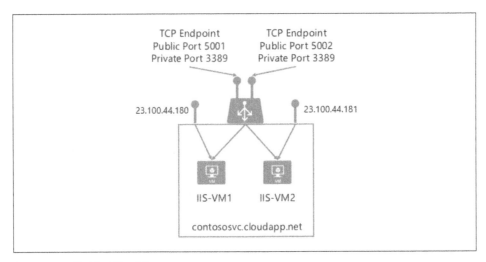

Figure 4-8. Public IP addresses

Using a public IP address puts the virtual machine directly on the Internet and out from behind the load balancer. This means that it is up to you to secure the ports on the virtual machine by using the built-in firewall in Windows Server or one of the various Linux-based solutions.

You can specify a new public IP address at virtual machine provisioning time or after the fact by using the update syntax along with the Set-AzurePublicIP cmdlet.

The partial example shown in Example 4-24 retrieves the current virtual machine configuration using the Get-AzureVM cmdlet and pipes it to the Set-AzurePublicIP cmdlet. The Set-AzurePublicIP cmdlet modifies the configuration to request a public IP using a unique name (in this case, the name of the virtual machine concatenated with -IP).

Example 4-24. Adding a public IP to an existing virtual machine

```
Get-AzureVM -ServiceName $serviceName -Name $vmName |
    Set-AzurePublicIP -PublicIPName "$vmName-IP" |
    Update-AzureVM
```

The same pattern applies to removing the public IP address from the virtual machine (see Example 4-25).

Example 4-25. Removing a public IP virtual machine using a public IP

```
Get-AzureVM -ServiceName $serviceName -Name $vmName |
    Remove-AzurePublicIP -PublicIPName "$vmName-IP" |
    Update-AzureVM
```

Summary

In this chapter you have learned how to use the Microsoft Azure PowerShell cmdlets to create and update network endpoints (including health probes), access control lists, reserved IP addresses, and public IP addresses. These are all critical techniques when it comes to automating a new deployment or performing updates across multiple virtual machines. Microsoft Azure virtual networks is another very important feature in the networking stack and will be discussed in Chapter 6. In the next chapter we will stay focused on automating virtual machine configuration and investigate storage in-depth.

## CHAPTER 5

Virtual Machine Storage

Storage Management

Microsoft Azure virtual machines are based on some of the same virtualization technologies in Windows Server Hyper-V. From a storage perspective, this means that the underlying disks and images are based on Microsoft Virtual Hard Disk (VHD) format. As you have seen in Chapter 3, virtual machine disks are stored in Microsoft Azure Storage, which itself is a highly scalable, durable, and available service. In this chapter we will dig deeper into how you can use PowerShell to manage these disks and configure storage for your virtual machines.

Uploading and Downloading VHDs

To start with, let's explore how to upload and download VHD files with Microsoft Azure storage. As you have already seen, it is possible to create VHD files in the cloud without the need to create them locally and upload them. However, I feel that starting at this point makes some of the concepts later in the chapter easier to explain.

The Microsoft Azure PowerShell cmdlets provide two cmdlets for uploading and downloading VHD files to a storage account: `Add-AzureVHD` and `Save-AzureVHD`. Let's explore each of these cmdlets using a simple walk-through.

Uploading a VHD

Using the Microsoft Azure PowerShell cmdlets over most generic storage tools has its advantages. In addition to easy scriptability, the cmdlets do not treat the VHD files as plain old blobs of data. Instead, the cmdlets have knowledge of the native VHD file format. This means that the cmdlets can optimize how they upload or download VHDs.

The Add-AzureVHD cmdlet supports an optimized upload. When you upload a VHD, the cmdlet evaluates which bytes of the file have data and transmits only the written bytes to storage while keeping the overall structure of the file intact.

Microsoft Azure currently supports only VHD files in fixed format. That does not mean that you have to convert your dynamic disks to fixed before uploading. The Add-AzureVHD cmdlet can dynamically convert from dynamic to fixed on upload. Unfortunately, at this time it does not support converting from VHDX to VHD, but that scenario can easily be accomplished with the Convert-VHD cmdlet that comes with Server 2012 R2 and Windows 8.1.

The Add-AzureVHD cmdlet supports three optional parameters shown in Table 5-1.

Table 5-1. Add-AzureVHD optional parameters

-OverWrite	If the VHD exists on the destination, you can overwrite it by passing this parameter.
-NumberOfThreads	The default value is 8. Change if you feel that more or less parallelization would improve your upload.
-BaseImageUriToPatch	When uploading a differencing disk, specify the image name to patch.

Authentication with the Add-AzureVHD and Save-AzureVHD cmdlets works the same way as the other Microsoft Azure cmdlets. You can call Select-AzureSubscription prior to their usage, and they will use the selected subscription and authentication method. As an alternative, shared access signatures are also fully supported. You can use a shared access signature by specifying it as part of the destination URL.

To try uploading a VHD on your own, create a new PowerShell script in the PowerShell ISE named *chapter5upload.ps1*. Add the code shown in Example 5-1 to the file. Ensure that you replace the placeholder values with real values. Do not execute the script yet because you still have to create the *mydatadisk.vhd* file using the disk management tool in Windows.

This example assumes that you have the virtual machine named ps-vm1 from Chapter 3 (feel free to substitute another virtual machine in its place).

Example 5-1. Using Add-AzureVHD to upload a VHD (Script pane)

```
$subscription = "[subscription name]"
$storageAccount = "[storage account name]"
$serviceName = "[cloud service name]"
$vmName = "ps-vm1"

Select-AzureSubscription $subscription

$source = "C:\VHDFiles\mydatadisk.vhd"
$destination = "https://$storageAccount.blob.core.windows.net/upload/mydatadisk.vhd"

Add-AzureVHD -LocalFilePath $source -Destination $destination

Add-AzureDisk -DiskName "mydatadisk" -MediaLocation $destination
```

```
Get-AzureVM -ServiceName $serviceName -Name $vmName |
    Add-AzureDataDisk -Import -DiskName "mydatadisk" -LUN 1 |
    Update-AzureVM
```

The call to the `Add-AzureDisk` cmdlet associates the VHD file with the mydatadisk disk name. Once the name is registered, you can easily attach or detach the disk by name using the `Add-AzureDataDisk` and `Remove-AzureDataDisk` cmdlets.

These cmdlets work by modifying the returned virtual machine configuration from `Get-AzureVM` by either adding or removing the referenced disk name. The modified configuration is then passed to `Update-AzureVM`, which in turn calls the appropriate API for passing the configuration to Azure to perform the update.

Creating a Local VHD with Windows

Before you can execute the script, you need to create the *VHDFiles* folder on the C: drive and the *mydatadisk.vhd* file. Using the built-in functionality in Windows 7 and above, you can create the VHD file locally, mount it, add data to it, and then upload it using the Azure cmdlets.

To do this on your own, open Control Panel→Administrative Tools, and then open Computer Management (see Figure 5-1).

Figure 5-1. Computer Management

When Computer Management is open, expand Storage, right-click Disk Configuration, and click Create VHD (see Figure 5-2).

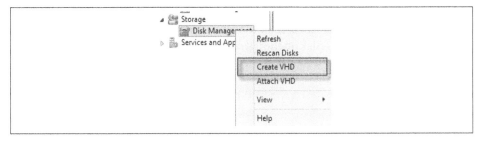

Figure 5-2. Create VHD

When the dialog opens, specify *C:\VHDFiles\mydatadisk.vhd* in the path (make sure you have created the *VHDFiles* folder first!) and specify 50 MB to keep the disk small but still usable. You should also ensure that VHD is selected and not VHDX before creating the VHD (see Figure 5-3).

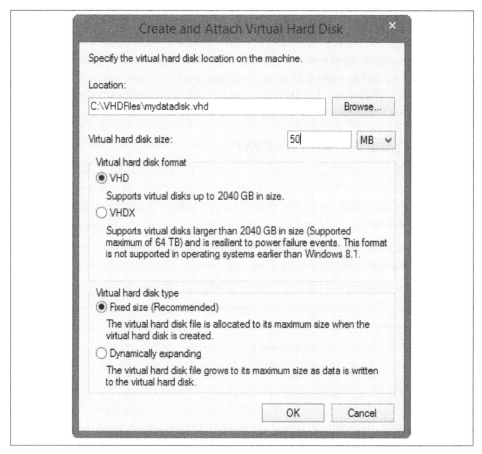

Figure 5-3. Specifying local VHD location

After the disk is created, you will then need to intialize and format it before adding data. To initialize the VHD, right-click on the left side (where it says Disk 1) and click Initialize Disk (see Figure 5-4). A new dialog will open; change the partition table format to MBR and click OK.

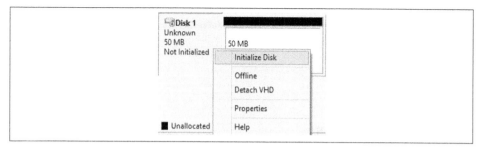

Figure 5-4. Initializing a disk

After the disk is initialized, right-click on the right side of the disk and select New Simple Volume. Accept the defaults for the New Simple Volume Wizard and let Windows format the drive (see Figure 5-5).

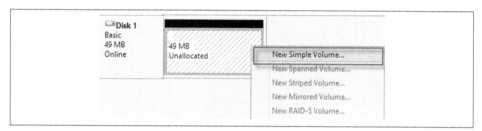

Figure 5-5. Creating a new simple volume

When the disk formatting has completed, open the new drive in File Explorer and put data of some kind on it (such as a simple text file). See Figure 5-6.

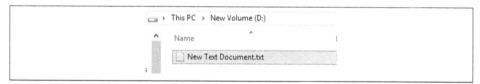

Figure 5-6. Adding data to the disk

Finally, detach the disk from Windows by going back to Computer Management→Storage→Disk Configuration, and then right-clicking on the new disk and selecting Detach VHD (see Figure 5-7).

Disk 1
Basic
49 MB
Online
New Volume (D:)
New Spanned Volume...
New Striped Volume...
New Mirrored Volume...
New RAID-5 Volume...
Convert to Dynamic Disk...
Convert to GPT Disk
Offline
Detach VHD

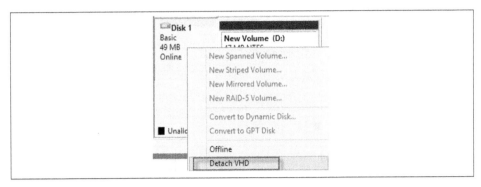

Figure 5-7. Detaching the VHD

You are now ready to upload the VHD and attach it to the virtual machine!

Execute the script by pressing F5 or by highlighting the script and pressing F8 to start the upload (see Figure 5-8).

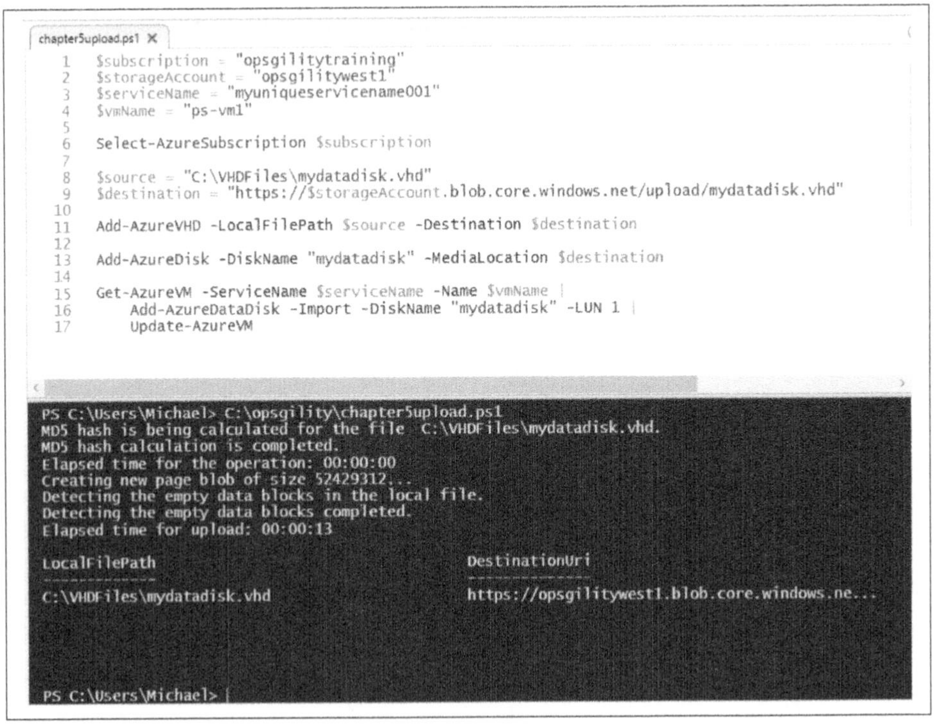

chapter5upload.ps1
$subscription = "opsgilitytraining"
$storageAccount = "opsgilitywest1"
$serviceName = "myuniqueservicename001"
$vmName = "ps-vm1"
Select-AzureSubscription $subscription
$source = "C:\VHDFiles\mydatadisk.vhd"
$destination = "https://$storageAccount.blob.core.windows.net/upload/mydatadisk.vhd"
Add-AzureVHD -LocalFilePath $source -Destination $destination
Add-AzureDisk -DiskName "mydatadisk" -MediaLocation $destination
Get-AzureVM -ServiceName $serviceName -Name $vmName |
Add-AzureDataDisk -Import -DiskName "mydatadisk" -LUN 1 |
Update-AzureVM
PS C:\Users\Michael> C:\opsgility\chapter5upload.ps1
MD5 hash is being calculated for the file C:\VHDFiles\mydatadisk.vhd.
MD5 hash calculation is completed.
Elapsed time for the operation: 00:00:00
Creating new page blob of size 52429312...
Detecting the empty data blocks in the local file.
Detecting the empty data blocks completed.
Elapsed time for upload: 00:00:13
LocalFilePath
DestinationUri
C:\VHDFiles\mydatadisk.vhd
https://opsgilitywest1.blob.core.windows.ne...
PS C:\Users\Michael>

Figure 5-8. Completing the upload

Validating the Disk

If you are following the exercise, the next step is to validate that the disk was actually uploaded and attached to the virtual machine (see Example 5-2). This step just requires you to log in using remote desktop via the Microsoft Azure management portal, or by using the Get-AzureRemoteDesktopFile cmdlet.

Example 5-2. Logging in to validate the attached disk (Console pane)

```
Get-AzureRemoteDesktopFile -ServiceName $serviceName -Name "ps-vm1" -Launch
```

When you are logged in, launch File Explorer and browse your disks. You should have a 49 to 50 MB disk attached with a simple file in it (see Figure 5-9).

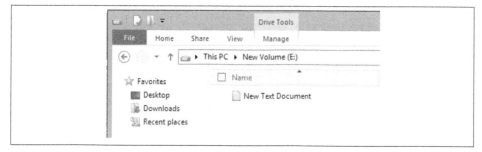

Figure 5-9. Validating the uploaded disk

At this point I like to modify the file with some changes. I do this because the next step is to download the VHD again, and I can validate the changes locally after the download.

Downloading a VHD

Downloading a VHD from Microsoft Azure with PowerShell is very similar to uploading, since the the the parameters are reversed from Add-AzureVHD. The source parameter is now the location of the VHD in storage, and the destination is the location on the local file system. To try this out on your own, create a new PowerShell script in the PowerShell ISE named *chapter5download.ps1* and add the code shown in Example 5-3.

Example 5-3. Downloading a VHD

```
$subscription = "[subscription name]"

$storageAccount = "[storage account name]"

Select-AzureSubscription $subscription

$destination = "C:\VHDFiles\mydatadisk_downloaded.vhd"

$source = "https://$storageAccount.blob.core.windows.net/upload/mydatadisk.vhd"
```

```
Save-AzureVhd -Source $source -LocalFilePath $destination
```

Press F5, or highlight the script and press F8 to execute the script (see Figure 5-10).

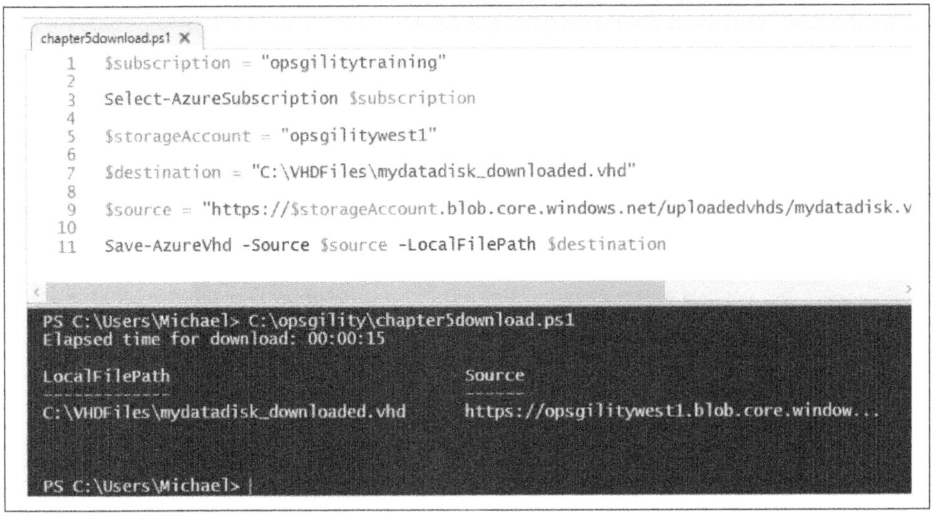

```
chapter5download.ps1 ✕
    1   $subscription = "opsgilitytraining"
    2
    3   Select-AzureSubscription $subscription
    4
    5   $storageAccount = "opsgilitywest1"
    6
    7   $destination = "C:\VHDFiles\mydatadisk_downloaded.vhd"
    8
    9   $source = "https://$storageAccount.blob.core.windows.net/uploadedvhds/mydatadisk.v
   10
   11   Save-AzureVhd -Source $source -LocalFilePath $destination

PS C:\Users\Michael> C:\opsgility\chapter5download.ps1
Elapsed time for download: 00:00:15

LocalFilePath                              Source
------------                               ------
C:\VHDFiles\mydatadisk_downloaded.vhd      https://opsgilitywest1.blob.core.window...


PS C:\Users\Michael> |
```

Figure 5-10. VHD download complete

When the VHD file is downloaded, you can double-click the downloaded file to mount it in Windows and examine the file for your changes.

Detaching a VHD
After you have mounted the VHD in Windows, you can't delete it until you first detach it by using Disk Configuration.

Save-AzureVHD Tips

There are some things you should know about downloading using the Save-AzureVHD cmdlet. First, if you attempt to download a VHD that is actively being written to, chances are very high that the operation will fail due to conflict between the new I/O from the virtual machine and the cmdlet downloading the written bytes.

The second thing you should know is that download is also optimized like the upload. The cmdlet will download only the written bytes of the VHD. However, the cmdlet currently does not support converting to a dynamic VHD on save and saves only to fixed disks. If the disk you are downloading is 1 TB in size but has only 50 GB written to it, the cmdlet will download only 50 GB but will require the full 1 TB of local storage to hold the file.

Similar to `Add-AzureVHD`, the `Save-AzureVHD` cmdlet supports the `-Overwrite` and `-NumberOfThreads` parameters. This cmdlet also supports a `-StorageKey` parameter that allows you to specify the authentication key for the storage account (see Table 5-2). If the key is not specified, the currently selected subscription is used to attempt authentication.

Table 5-2. Save-AzureVHD optional parameters

-OverWrite	If the VHD exists on the destination, you can overwrite it by passing this parameter.
-NumberOfThreads	Default value is 8. Change if you feel that more or less parallelization would improve your download.
-StorageKey	The authentication key to the storage account.

Disks and Images

Virtual machine VHD files are referenced indirectly through disks and images in Microsoft Azure. Disks and images are named entities that contain metadata and a link to the underlying VHD.

What Is an Image?

In Microsoft Azure an *image* is a named entity that is mapped to an operating system disk and optionally a set of data disks. Images are used to instantiate virtual machines with a specific operating system with or without customizations applied. Images can reside in the Microsoft Azure image gallery if they are part of the platform, or they can reside in a storage account in your own subscription if they are your own custom images. Images are designed to be a customized version of what a virtual machine should look like.

There are two types of images that can be created. The original image type is called an *OS image*. This image type can reference only the operating system disk and works only with images that have been generalized with Sysprep or the Linux Waagent. The second image type is called a *virtual machine (VM) image*. This image type can reference data disks in addition to the operating system disk and can be generalized or specialized.

A VM image that has been generalized is used for creating multiple virtual machine instances with the same starting point. These virtual machines will be customized with their own computer names at provision time. A specialized VM image is not generalized. This means that it will retain its own identity such as a computer name and even domain-join information. This image type is especially useful for taking backups of a specific virtual machine for development and test, or as a general-purpose backup solution at the VHD level. It is very similar in concept to exporting a virtual machine in Hyper-V. A key difference is that you have to take special care to shut the virtual machine down, because currently the image creation process does not freeze the state of your applications before capture.

To register a VHD file as an image, the VHD file must first be in a Microsoft Azure storage account. Whether it was uploaded there or copied from another location (we'll talk about this capability a bit later) doesn't really matter. To register a VHD file located in a storage account, simply call the `Add-AzureVMImage` cmdlet.

For example, let's assume that you have previously used the `Add-AzureVHD` cmdlet to upload the *myWindowsImage.vhd* file to your storage account in the *upload* container. The call to `Add-AzureVMImage` creates the image named MyWinImage that is backed by the file you uploaded, and it is marked as being a Windows-based virtual machine (see Example 5-4). Specifying the OS on the image is important because Linux and Windows have distinct provisioning processes for creating a new virtual machine instance from a generalized image.

Example 5-4. Registering an operating system image

```
$storageAccount = "[storage account name]"
$source = "https://$storageAccount.blob.core.windows.net/upload/myWindowsImage.vhd"
$imageName = "MyWinImage"

Add-AzureVMImage -ImageName $imageName -MediaLocation $source -OS Windows
```

What Is a Disk?

A Microsoft Azure *disk* is another entity mapped to a VHD file in Microsoft Azure. Unlike an image, it is never generalized and it is not required to have an operating system on it, as it could just hold data. A disk with an operating system is called an *OS disk*, and one is created each time you create a virtual machine from an image. A disk without an operating system in Microsoft Azure is a *data disk*. These are meant to hold exactly what you would expect to be on a data disk: data.

Example 5-5 is a simple example of how you could register two previously created or uploaded VHD files in your subscription as usable disks. The first call to `Add-AzureDisk` registers the *myosdrive.vhd* as an OS disk by specifying the `-OS Windows` parameter to the cmdlet.

The second call to `Add-AzureDisk` registers a simple data disk. When execution is complete, this disk could then be attached to a virtual machine at provision time or to a virtual machine that already exists.

Example 5-5. Registering an OS and data disk

```
$storageAccount = "[storage account name]"
$osdisk = "https://$storageAccount.blob.core.windows.net/upload/myosdrive.vhd"
$osdiskName = "os disk"
```

```
$datadisk = "https://$storageAccount.blob.core.windows.net/upload/mydatadrive.vhd"
$datadiskname = "data disk"

# Register the operating system disk
Add-AzureDisk -DiskName $osdiskName -MediaLocation $osdisk -OS Windows

# Register the data disk
Add-AzureDisk -DiskName $datadiskname -MediaLocation $datadisk
```

Creating a virtual machine from disks is similar to creating a virtual machine from an image, with just a few differences.

The first difference is you need to specify the OS disk name to the -DiskName parameter on New-AzureVMConfig instead of an ImageName. The second difference is when creating a virtual machine from a disk, you do not need to use the Add-AzureProvisioningConfig cmdlet to populate the provisioning configuration. The provisioning configuration data is used only with a generalized image. The third change is regarding attaching the data disk. Instead of using the -CreateNew parameter with Add-AzureDataDisk, you specify -Import and the name of the data disk with the -DiskName parameter (see Example 5-6).

Example 5-6. Creating a virtual machine from a disk

```
$serviceName = "[cloud service name]"
$location = "[region name]"
$vmName = "migratedVM"
$vmSize = "Small"
$osdiskName = "os disk"
$datadiskname = "data disk"

# Create the configuration specifying the disk name instead of an image
$vmConfig = New-AzureVMConfig -Name $vmName `
                              -InstanceSize $vmSize `
                              -DiskName $osdiskName

# Import the data disk to the first LUN
$vmConfig | Add-AzureDataDisk -Import -DiskName $datadiskname -LUN 0

# Create the virtual machine
$vmConfig | New-AzureVM -ServiceName $serviceName -Location $location
```

Managing Images

Now that you understand the basics of images and disks, I want to dig deeper into each of these entities, starting with images.

There are cmdlets to help you manage images. We have seen one of them in Chapter 3 (Get-AzureVMImage), and we have also just seen how to register an image based on a VHD using the `Add-AzureVMImage` cmdlet. Let's investigate some of the additional options you have with managing virtual machine images.

Viewing Image Properties

Running `Get-AzureVMImage` on its own will give you a list of all of the platform images and user images available to your subscription.

Each image has a list of properties that can be filtered on using PowerShell (see Table 5-3). For custom images that you create, some of these properties can also be set with the `Set-AzureVMImage` cmdlet.

Table 5-3. Image properties

Category	Public (Microsoft Azure images) or User (your images).
Location	The location(s) where the image is usable.
LogicalSizeInGB	The size of the image (and the size your OS disk will be).
Label	Descriptive label.
MediaLink	Full URI to the underlying VHD. Ths is applicable only to User images.
ImageName	The name of the image. This is the value passed to create a virtual machine.
OS	Whether the OS is Windows or Linux.
OSDiskConfiguration	Configuration of the operating system disk.
DataDiskConfigurations	Configuration of the captured data disks (if any).
Eula	End-user license agreement for the image.
Description	Descriptive text.
ImageFamily	A logical grouping of images (SQL, Server 2012 R2, etc.)
PublishedDate	When the image was made available.
IsPremium	If True, there will be an additional usage charge on top of compute.
IconUri	URI to the icon for the image that will show up in the portal.
PrivacyUri	URI to the privacy policy for the image.
RecommendedVMSize	Recommended virtual machine size for the image.
PublisherName	Name of the group or company that published the image.

Filtering images by using these properties is simple with PowerShell. For instance, if you would like to see all of the images that charge a premium on top of the regular compute hours, run the command shown in Example 5-7.

Example 5-7. Filtering on only premium images

```
Get-AzureVMImage | where { $_.IsPremium -eq $true }
```

With PowerShell, you can combine these filters to make more-advanced queries. Example 5-8 shows filtering on only premium images that recommend the A6 instance size.

Example 5-8. Filtering on only premium images and recommended virtual machine size

```
Get-AzureVMImage |
        where { $_.IsPremium -eq $true -and $_.RecommendedVMSize -eq "A6" }
```

The only value you will use from a virtual machine image to create a virtual machine is the `ImageName` property. It is useful to know how to select only that property when querying images, as shown in Example 5-9.

Example 5-9. Filtering on only premium images and selecting ImageName

```
Get-AzureVMImage | where { $_.IsPremium -eq $true } | select ImageName
```

In Chapter 3 I showed how you can use the filtering capabilities to return the image by publish date so you always get the latest version with the latest patches (see Example 5-10).

Example 5-10. Filtering by image publish date

```
$imageName = Get-AzureVMImage |
                where { $_.ImageFamily -eq $imageFamily } |
                sort PublishedDate -Descending |
                select -ExpandProperty ImageName -First 1
```

If you would like to view images that are specialized, you can filter on the `OSState` property of the `OSDiskConfiguration` property. This value can be `Specialized` or `Generalized` (see Example 5-11).

Example 5-11. Filtering only specialized images

```
Get-AzureVMImage | where { $_.OSDiskConfiguration.OSState -eq "Specialized" }
```

Capturing a Generalized Image

Now that you know how to view and filter images, how do you create one of your own? To create a custom image, let's walk through the steps from the very beginning by creating a new virtual machine, customizing it, and then capturing it as an image.

The image capture process works by starting with a base virtual machine. When the virtual machine is booted, you customize it (install software, make configuration changes, and so on) to make the virtual machine exactly how you want new virtual machines to start.

When the virtual machine is customized, you then run the tool to generalize the operating system. In Windows, you use the Sysprep tool. In Linux, you can use the Microsoft

Azure agent (Waagent) to accomplish a similar task. This step prepares the operating system in the same way that OEMs do after installing software on a new computer. When the virtual machine boots up, it will go through the provisioning process just like a new install of Windows would, except your changes will already be on the virtual machine. As you can imagine, this is a fairly destructive process, so read the documentation for any applications you are considering imaging. SQL Server and SharePoint are just two examples of applications that support Sysprep but have very specific instructions on how to accomplish it in a supported manner.

Finally, after you have successfully run Sysprep and the virtual machine is shut down, you can then capture the virtual machine as an image. Capturing a generalized image also deletes the virtual machine instance that was captured, as it no longer has a machine name and requires going through the full provisioning process to be useful again. You now have the saved image stored in a storage account to allow you to easily provision one or more instances of the virtual machine that you captured.

Hopefully, the imaging process is a little more clear to you now if it was not already. With that in mind, let's use PowerShell to create an image (we'll cheat ever so slightly by using remote desktop to customize the virtual machine, but I'll show how you can script that in Chapter 7).

Creating the virtual machine

Using the PowerShell ISE, create a new script named *chapter5vmimage.ps1* and add the code shown in Example 5-12. Make sure to replace all of the placeholder values with correct values. For this example, ensure that your cloud service name is globally unique.

Example 5-12. Creating a virtual machine for imaging (Script pane)

```
$subscription = "[subscription name]"
Select-AzureSubscription $subscription

# Specify the admin credentials
$adminUser = "[admin username]"
$password = "[admin password]"

$location = "[region name]"
$serviceName = "[cloud service name]"

$vmName = "ps-vmImage"
$vmSize = "Small"
$imageFamily = "Windows Server 2012 R2 Datacenter"

$imageName = Get-AzureVMImage |
                where { $_.ImageFamily -eq $imageFamily } |
                sort PublishedDate -Descending |
                select -ExpandProperty ImageName -First 1

New-AzureQuickVM -Windows `
```

```
              -ServiceName $serviceName `
              -Name $vmName `
              -ImageName $imageName `
              -Location $location `
              -AdminUsername $adminUser `
              -Password $password `
              -InstanceSize $vmSize `
              -WaitForBoot
```

In this example I have also introduced the -WaitForBoot flag. This flag ensures that New-AzureQuickVM (or New-AzureVM) does not return until the virtual machine is in the ReadyRole state. This makes it very convenient to know when you can log in to the virtual machine or execute a script remotely to customize the virtual machine.

Customizing the virtual machine

Next, run the code shown in Example 5-13 to launch a remote desktop session into the virtual machine.

Example 5-13. Launching a Remote Desktop into the virtual machine for customization (Console pane)

```
Get-AzureRemoteDesktopFile -ServiceName $serviceName -Name $vmName -Launch
```

When prompted, enter the username and password specified in your script to log in. When you are logged in to the newly created virtual machine, click the Windows PowerShell icon on the task bar.

The whole point of creating an image is that you would like the ability to create multiple instances of a virtual machine that has a preexisting configuration on it. In this case, we can install IIS so that we can easily deploy a web server using the custom image.

Launch PowerShell, and at the PowerShell command line on the virtual machine, execute the command shown in Example 5-14 to install IIS (see Figure 5-11).

Example 5-14. Installing IIS on the new virtual machine (Console pane)

```
Add-WindowsFeature -Name "Web-Server" -IncludeAllSubFeature -IncludeManagementTools
```

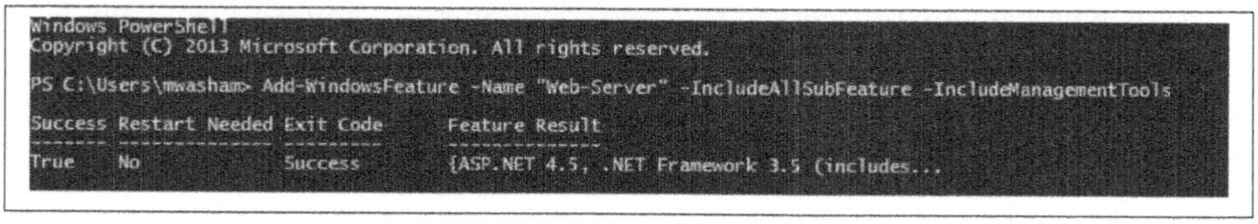

Figure 5-11. Installing IIS using PowerShell

When all customizations for your image have been made (which in this case is just installing the Web-Server feature), the next step is to run Sysprep.

Running Sysprep on the virtual machine

Within the virtual machine, press Windows Key + R and enter `C:\Windows\Sys tem32\Sysprep\sysprep.exe` as the command to run, and press Enter. See Figure 5-12.

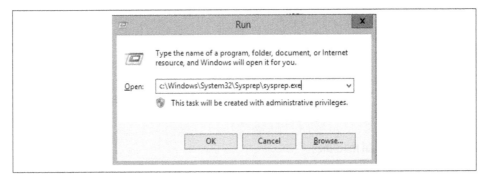

Figure 5-12. Starting Sysprep

When the Sysprep wizard is displayed on the screen, as shown in Figure 5-13, check the Generalize checkbox and change Shutdown Options to Shutdown, and then click OK.

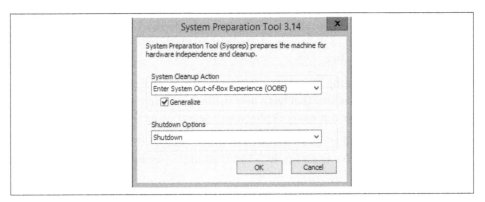

Figure 5-13. Configuring Sysprep

The system preparation process can take several minutes to complete. Eventually, your remote desktop session will be stopped (this is supposed to happen), and the next step is to wait until the virtual machine is in the `StoppedVM` state. You can check this by running the `Get-AzureVM` cmdlet to view the virtual machine's status.

Capturing the virtual machine image

When the virtual machine is stopped, you can capture the image by using the Microsoft Azure management portal or with PowerShell.

Run the code shown in Example 5-15 in the console of the PowerShell ISE. I have split the call to `Save-AzureVMImage` across multiple lines for clarity, but it can be executed on one line by removing the line continuation character (`` ` ``). This example creates a new virtual machine image and saves it in the storage account where the virtual machine disks are currently located.

Example 5-15. Capturing and setting properties of an image (Console pane)

```
$imageName = "WEBSERVERIMAGE"
$imageLabel = "Image with IIS Pre-Installed"

Save-AzureVMImage -ServiceName $serviceName `
                  -Name $vmName `
                  -NewImageName $imageName `
                  -NewImageLabel $imageLabel `
                  -OSState Generalized
```

Provisioning a virtual machine from your own image

To create a virtual machine using this new image, create a new script using the PowerShell ISE named *chapter5createfromimage.ps1* and enter the code shown in Example 5-16. Ensure that you replace the placeholder values with real ones from your subscription.

Example 5-16. Creating a virtual machine from the image (Script pane)

```
$subscription = "[subscription name]"
$location = "[region name]"
$serviceName = "[cloud service name]"

# Specify the admin credentials
$adminUser = "[admin username]"
$password = "[admin password]"

Select-AzureSubscription $subscription
$vmSize = "Small"
$vmName = "ps-webserver1"

$imageName = "WEBSERVERIMAGE"

New-AzureQuickVM -Windows `
                 -ServiceName $serviceName `
                 -Name $vmName `
                 -ImageName $imageName `
                 -Location $location `
                 -AdminUsername $adminUser `
                 -Password $password `
                 -InstanceSize $vmSize
```

Updating a Virtual Machine Image

When the image is created, there are two pieces of the image that you may want to modify in the future.

The first is the properties of the virtual machine image entity in Microsoft Azure. To update the properties, use the Update-AzureVMImage cmdlet along with the image name.

To try this on your own, create a new script called *chapter5updateimage.ps1* and add the code shown in Example 5-17.

Example 5-17. Updating a virtual machine image (Script pane)

```
$subscription = "[subscription name]"
Select-AzureSubscription $subscription

$imageName = "WEBSERVERIMAGE"

Update-AzureVMImage -ImageName $imageName `
                    -Description "A Pre-Built web server" `
                    -ImageFamily "My Company Custom Images - IIS" `
                    -Label "Image with IIS Pre-Installed"
```

Execute the script by pressing F5, or by highlighting the text and pressing F8 to update the image.

Execute the Get-AzureVMImage cmdlet to verify your changes (see Example 5-18).

Example 5-18. Verifying the properties (Console pane)

```
$imageName = "WEBSERVERIMAGE"

Get-AzureVMImage -ImageName $imageName
```

The second type of update is to update the underlying image bits themselves. This can be accomplished in one of two ways. The first and likely the simplest way is to create a new virtual machine instance from the image, and then update the virtual machine by applying patches and software updates. When the virtual machine instance is updated, run Sysprep again and capture the image with a new name.

The alternative method assumes that you have created the image offline and uploaded it using the Add-AzureVHD cmdlet. If you have, then you can create differencing disks offline with the updates and upload only the differencing disks and have them applied to the base image using the Add-AzureVHD cmdlet and specifying the image URL with the -BaseImageUriToPatch parameter.

Deleting a Virtual Machine Image

Deleting a custom image is straightforward with the `Remove-AzureVMImage` cmdlet. `Remove-AzureVMImage` accepts two parameters: the `-ImageName` and, optionally, the `-DeleteVHD` parameter.

Example 5-19 will delete the custom virtual machine image just created and, with the `-DeleteVHD` parameter added, will also delete the underlying VHD in your storage account.

Example 5-19. Deleting a custom image (Console pane)

```
Remove-AzureVMImage -ImageName $imageName -DeleteVHD
```

OS Images and VM Images

The original imaging technology that was released when Microsoft shipped virtual machines is known as *OS images*. Since then, a new imaging architecture has been released and this new architecture is known as *VM images*. The biggest difference between OS images and VM images is that VM images can also capture data disks. The second difference is that VM images also support capturing specialized images (see Table 5-4). This support for specialized images means you can create a virtual machine and capture it without running Sysprep or Waagent (Linux), and the OS disk and data disks will be captured as is, including the unique identity of the VM.

Table 5-4. Image type comparison

OS image	VM image
OS disk only	OS and data disks
Generalized only	Generalized or specialized

The `Save-AzureVMImage` cmdlet can be used to create each image type.

To create an OS image, simply omit the `-OSState` parameter, and the image will be created as an OS image, as shown in Example 5-20. This is an important point to remember, because if you were anticipating capturing data disks, you will be disappointed if you forget to specify the `-OSState` parameter.

Example 5-20. Creating an OS image (no data disks included)

```
$serviceName = "[cloud service name]"
$vmName = "[virtual machine name]"
$imageName = "[image name]"
$imageLabel = "[image label]"

Save-AzureVMImage -ServiceName $serviceName `
                  -Name $vmName `
                  -NewImageName $imageName `
                  -NewImageLabel $imageLabel
```

Accidently losing data disks

Calling `Save-AzureVMImage` without the `-OSState` parameter reverts to using the OS image type, which does not support data disks.

Specifying the `-OSState Generalized` parameter creates a VM image, and if there are data disks associated with the virtual machine, they will be captured as well (see Example 5-21). Using this parameter assumes that the virtual machine has been generalized with Sysprep on Windows or the Microsoft Azure Linux agent (Waagent).

Example 5-21. Creating a generalized virtual machine image

```
$serviceName = "[cloud service name]"
$vmName = "[virtual machine name]"
$imageName = "[image name]"
$imageLabel = "[image label]"

Save-AzureVMImage  -ServiceName $serviceName `
                   -Name $vmName `
                   -NewImageName $imageName `
                   -NewImageLabel $imageLabel `
                   -OSState Generalized
```

Specifying the `-OSState Specialized` parameter creates a VM image, and if there are data disks associated with the virtual machine, they will be captured as well (see Example 5-22). Using this parameter assumes that the virtual machine has *not* been generalized with Sysprep on Windows or the Azure Linux agent (Waagent). This scenario is great for capturing a virtual machine exactly how it should be when deployed. An example is creating an image of the virtual machine before applying updates or an application deployment. If the update or deployment fails, you can delete the virtual machine and re-create it from the image, and the state will be exactly as it was before provisioning.

Example 5-22. Creating a specialized virtual machine image

```
$serviceName = "[cloud service name]"
$vmName = "[virtual machine name]"
$imageName = "[image name]"
$imageLabel = "[image label]"

Save-AzureVMImage  -ServiceName $serviceName `
                   -Name $vmName `
                   -NewImageName $imageName `
                   -NewImageLabel $imageLabel `
                   -OSState Specialized
```

Shutdown for a clean image capture

Before creating a specialized image, it is a good idea to shut the virtual machine down first to ensure that all writes to the disks are flushed before capture. When creating a generalized image, the VM is already shut down due to the generalization process. With the specialization option, it is up to you whether you want to shut down the virtual machine first.

Managing Disks

As you now know, a disk is similar in concept to an image. It is an entity in Microsoft Azure that is backed by a VHD file in a storage account. The VHD file can be a bootable OS disk with a supported version of Windows or Linux on it or it can be a simple data disk that contains only data.

When you create a virtual machine from an image, a copy of that image is made to the target location you specified for your virtual machine, and this becomes the OS disk.

Just like images, there are additional cmdlets to help you manage your disks. You have already seen how to attach a new disk to a virtual machine by using `Add-AzureDataDisk` with the `-CreateNew` parameter, and you have seen how to register a VHD file to a Microsoft Azure disk by using the `Add-AzureDisk` cmdlet. In this section we will dig deeper and show more scenarios for how disks can be managed using PowerShell.

OS Disks

An OS disk is simply a disk that contains a bootable operating system on it, and the OS property of the disk entity is set to Windows or Linux. An OS disk is created each time you create a virtual machine from an image or when you add an existing VHD to storage and register it by calling the `Add-AzureDisk` cmdlet with the `-OS` parameter specified.

In this partial example, shown in Example 5-23, the `$mediaLocation` variable points to a previously uploaded VHD in a storage account. To make this VHD usable to a virtual machine, the `Add-AzureDisk` cmdlet is used to create the disk entity that is mapped to the underlying VHD in storage. The `-OS Windows` parameter is also specified to register the disk as a Windows OS disk.

Example 5-23. Adding an OS disk

```
$mediaLocation = "https://$storageAccount.blob.windows.net/upload/myosdisk.vhd"

Add-AzureDisk -DiskLabel "My OS disk" -MediaLocation $mediaLocation -OS Windows
```

Data Disks

A data disk is similar to an OS disk except that it does not have an OS property specified. Microsoft Azure uses this property to decide whether the disk can be booted or just attached to a virtual machine.

As we have seen in Chapter 3, using the PowerShell cmdlets makes it easy to create additional empty disks to a virtual machine with up to 1023 GB in storage.

In this partial example, shown in Example 5-24, the $vmConfig variable is a virtual machine configuration object. It is piped to the Add-AzureDataDisk cmdlet, which has the -CreateNew parameter specified. The -CreateNew parameter makes the Add-AzureDataDisk cmdlet populate the configuration object with properties that, when sent to the Microsoft Azure API, will create new empty disks on the virtual machine.

Example 5-24. Attaching new data disks to a virtual machine configuation

```
$vmConfig | Add-AzureDataDisk -CreateNew `
                              -DiskSizeInGB 50 `
                              -DiskLabel "data 1" `
                              -LUN 0

$vmConfig | Add-AzureDataDisk -CreateNew `
                              -DiskSizeInGB 50 `
                              -DiskLabel "data 2" `
                              -LUN 1
```

Besides creating a new disk with the -CreateNew parameter, you can also attach existing disks by using the -Import or -ImportFrom parameters. This can be a disk that you have uploaded previously or other data disks that were created in Azure on other virtual machines. One thing to remember is that a disk cannot be attached to multiple virtual machines at the same time.

In this partial example, shown in Example 5-25, a data disk is created with the Add-AzureDisk cmdlet using the MyDataDisk name and the URL to an existing VHD in an Azure storage account. The -Import parameter of Add-AzureDataDisk allows you to just specify the disk name and attach it to a virtual machine.

Example 5-25. Importing a data disk by name

```
$mediaLocation = "https://$storageAccount.blob.windows.net/upload/mydatadisk.vhd"

Add-AzureDisk -DiskName "MyDataDisk" -MediaLocation $mediaLocation


$vmConfig | Add-AzureDataDisk -Import `
                              -DiskName "MyDataDisk" `
                              -LUN 0
```

Example 5-26 shows that it is also possible to specify an existing VHD in a storage account that is in the same subscription and same region by using the `Add-AzureDataDisk` cmdlet with the `-ImportFrom parameters` parameter. What does `-ImportFrom` actually mean? When you specify the `-ImportFrom` parameter and a storage account URI to a VHD, the cmdlet will automatically register the VHD as a disk and add it to your virtual machine configuration. This is a shortcut that is the same as calling `Add-AzureDisk` to register the disk and using the `-Import` parameter to add it to the virtual machine configuration at the same time.

Example 5-26. Importing a VHD as a data disk

```
$mediaLocation = "https://$storageAccount.blob.windows.net/upload/mydatadisk.vhd"

$vmConfig | Add-AzureDataDisk -ImportFrom `
                              -DiskLabel "imported vhd" `
                              -LUN 0 `
                              -MediaLocation $mediaLocation
```

Viewing Disk Properties

To view disks in your Azure subsription or to view the properties of a specific disk (listed in Table 5-5), you can use the `Get-AzureDisk` cmdlet. Running `Get-AzureDisk` with no parameters will return all of the disks in your subscription (see Example 5-27).

Example 5-27. Viewing disk properties (Console pane)

```
Get-AzureDisk
```

Table 5-5. Disk properties

AffinityGroup	The affinity group (if any) of the parent storage account.
AttachedTo	The virtual machine that the disk is attached to (null if not attached).
IsCorrupted	Whether corruption has been detected on the VHD.
Label	Descriptive label.
Location	The Microsoft Azure region (if not affinity group) of the parent storage account.
DiskSizeInGB	The size, in gigabytes, of the disk.
MediaLink	Full URI to the underlying VHD.
DiskName	The name of the disk. This is the value passed to any disk-related API.
SourceImageName	Source image name if the disk was created by an image.
OS	Windows or Linux if an OS disk or null if a data disk.

`Get-AzureDisk` also supports specifying just the `-DiskName` parameter if you would like to return only properties of a specific disk.

As with images, you can filter on the properties of disks. Example 5-28 calls `Get-AzureDisk` to return all of the disks from your subscription. The output of

`Get-AzureDisk` is piped to the `where` command, which filters the results further by including only disks where the `AttachedTo` property equals `null` (not mounted to a virtual machine) and OS equals `null` (not an operating system disk).

Example 5-28. Viewing only unattached data disks (Console pane)

```
Get-AzureDisk | where { $_.AttachedTo -eq $null -and $_.OS -eq $null }
```

Example 5-29 is another example of using the PowerShell filtering abilities. The commands are almost identical, except for filtering by a different value of the operating system. These commands may or may not return any data, depending on whether you have unattached OS disks for Windows or Linux in your current subscription.

Example 5-29. Viewing by operating system (Console pane)

```
Get-AzureDisk | where { $_.AttachedTo -eq $null -and $_.OS -eq "Windows" }

Get-AzureDisk | where { $_.AttachedTo -eq $null -and $_.OS -eq "Linux" }
```

Specifying Disk Locations at VM Creation

Under the covers, the PowerShell cmdlets automatically set the location of the disk to be in the storage account you specified with the `-CurrentStorageAccountName` parameter of the `Set-AzureSubscription` cmdlet and the default container vhds. Using the PowerShell cmdlets, you have the power to override this default behavior and have full control over the location and filenames of the VHDs, including the OS disk, by specifying the `-MediaLocation` parameter.

Example 5-30 is a full example. I am using the `-MediaLocation` parameter to specify the location of the underlying disks of a virtual machine when it is created. The `-MediaLocation` parameter is specified in the call to `New-AzureVMConfig` to override the location of the operating system disk, and each call to `Add-AzureDataDisk` specifies the location of each data disk.

If you would like to try this example on your own, create a new PowerShell script using the PowerShell ISE named *chapter5medialocation.ps1*.

Example 5-30. Creating a virtual machine with data disks (Script pane)

```
$subscription = "[subscription name]"
Select-AzureSubscription $subscription

$location = "[region name]"
$serviceName = "[cloud service name]"

# Specify the admin credentials
$adminUser = "[admin username]"
$password = "[admin password]"
```

```
$storageAccount = (Get-AzureSubscription -Current).CurrentStorageAccountName

$vmName = "ps-vmDisks"
$vmSize = "Small"

$imageFamily = "Windows Server 2012 R2 Datacenter"

$imageName = Get-AzureVMImage |
                where { $_.ImageFamily -eq $imageFamily } |
                sort PublishedDate -Descending |
                select -ExpandProperty ImageName -First 1

# Custom location and filenames
$oslocation = "https://$storageAccount.blob.core.windows.net/custom/osdisk.vhd"
$d1Location = "https://$storageAccount.blob.core.windows.net/custom/data1.vhd"
$d2Location = "https://$storageAccount.blob.core.windows.net/custom/data2.vhd"


$vmConfig = New-AzureVMConfig -Name $vmName `
                              -InstanceSize $vmSize `
                              -ImageName $imageName `
                              -MediaLocation $oslocation

$vmConfig | Add-AzureProvisioningConfig -Windows `
                              -AdminUsername $adminUser `
                              -Password $password

$vmConfig | Add-AzureDataDisk -CreateNew `
                              -DiskSizeInGB 50 `
                              -DiskLabel "data 1" `
                              -LUN 0 `
                              -MediaLocation $d1Location


$vmConfig | Add-AzureDataDisk -CreateNew `
                              -DiskSizeInGB 50 `
                              -DiskLabel "data 2" `
                              -LUN 1 `
                              -MediaLocation $d2Location

$vmConfig | New-AzureVM -ServiceName $serviceName -Location $location
```

Press F5, or highlight the script and press F8 to create the virtual machine. You can then use the Get-AzureVM cmdlet to return the virtual machine configuration and pipe it to Get-AzureOSDisk or Get-AzureDataDisk to view the custom media location (see Figures 5-14 and 5-15).

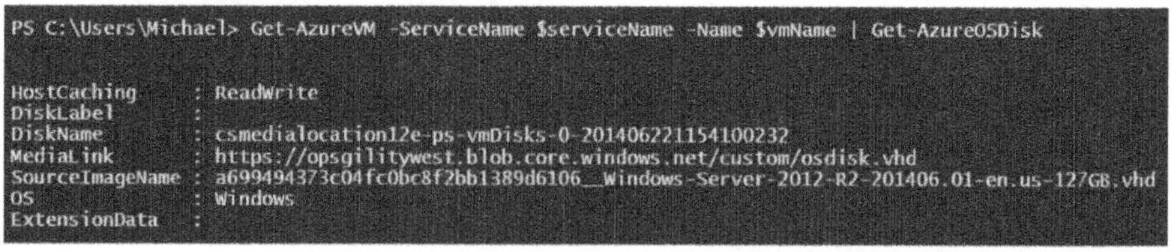

```
PS C:\Users\Michael> Get-AzureVM -ServiceName $serviceName -Name $vmName | Get-AzureOSDisk

HostCaching      : ReadWrite
DiskLabel        :
DiskName         : csmedialocation12e-ps-vmDisks-0-201406221154100232
MediaLink        : https://opsgilitywest.blob.core.windows.net/custom/osdisk.vhd
SourceImageName  : a699494373c04fc0bc8f2bb1389d6106__Windows-Server-2012-R2-201406.01-en.us-127GB.vhd
OS               : Windows
ExtensionData    :
```

Figure 5-14. Custom OS disk media location

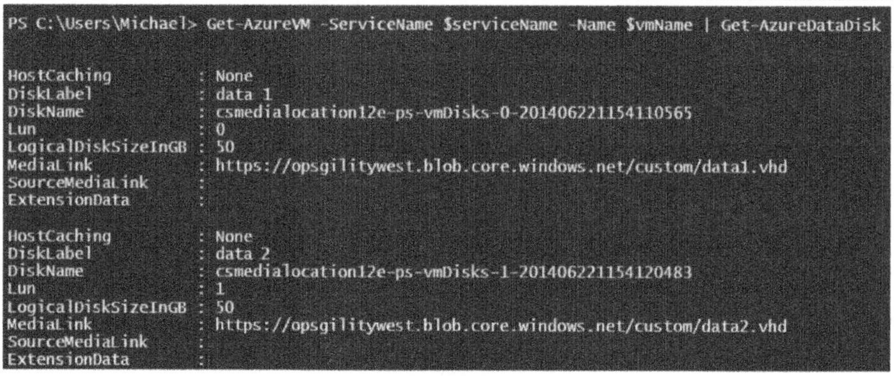

```
PS C:\Users\Michael> Get-AzureVM -ServiceName $serviceName -Name $vmName | Get-AzureDataDisk

HostCaching        : None
DiskLabel          : data 1
DiskName           : csmedialocation12e-ps-vmDisks-0-201406221154110565
Lun                : 0
LogicalDiskSizeInGB : 50
MediaLink          : https://opsgilitywest.blob.core.windows.net/custom/data1.vhd
SourceMediaLink    :
ExtensionData      :

HostCaching        : None
DiskLabel          : data 2
DiskName           : csmedialocation12e-ps-vmDisks-1-201406221154120483
Lun                : 1
LogicalDiskSizeInGB : 50
MediaLink          : https://opsgilitywest.blob.core.windows.net/custom/data2.vhd
SourceMediaLink    :
ExtensionData      :
```

Figure 5-15. Custom data disk media location

Specifying Cache

By default, ReadWrite caching is enabled on the OS disk of a virtual machine for performance. This means that most reads and writes to the C: drive are cached on the
physical disk that the virtual machine is hosted on before being committed to the disk
backed in Microsoft Azure storage. You can change the setting of the OS disk during
disk creation by specifying the -HostCaching parameter to New-AzureVMConfig, or use
the Set-AzureOSDisk cmdlet for changing the cache setting on an existing virtual machine's OS disk.

OS disk cache settings

Supported -HostCaching values for the OS disk are ReadOnly and
ReadWrite.

Up to four data disks per virtual machine can be enabled for disk caching. The default
cache setting of a data disk is None and is most likely the safest bet if you are actively
writing data to the disk. However, some workloads can be optimized by enabling local

read or write cache on the disk. During creation, you can specify the cache settings of a data disk with the -HostCaching flag of the Add-AzureDataDisk cmdlet, or use the Set-AzureDataDisk cmdlet to change the cache configuration on an existing virtual machine.

Data disk cache settings

Supported -HostCaching flag values for the OS disk are None, ReadOnly, and ReadWrite.

Example 5-31 is a partial example that shows how you can specify the -HostCaching parameter during creation to change the default cache behavior of OS and data disks.

Example 5-31. Specifying disk HostCaching during creation

```
# -HostCaching on New-AzureVMConfig refers to the OS disk setting
$vmConfig = New-AzureVMConfig -Name $vmName `
                              -InstanceSize $vmSize `
                              -ImageName $imageName `
                              -HostCaching ReadOnly

$vmConfig | Add-AzureProvisioningConfig -Windows `
                              -AdminUsername $adminUser `
                              -Password $password

$vmConfig | Add-AzureDataDisk -CreateNew `
                              -DiskSizeInGB 50 `
                              -DiskLabel "data 1" `
                              -LUN 0 `
                              -HostCaching ReadWrite

$vmConfig | Add-AzureDataDisk -CreateNew `
                              -DiskSizeInGB 50 `
                              -DiskLabel "data 2" `
                              -HostCaching ReadWrite
                              -LUN 1
```

Example 5-32 is a partial example that shows changing the -HostCaching property of an existing virtual machine's disks using the Set-AzureOSDisk and Set-AzureDataDisk cmdlets.

Example 5-32. Specifying HostCaching properties on an existing virtual machine

```
$vmConfig = Get-AzureVM -ServiceName $serviceName -Name $vmName

$vmConfig | Set-AzureOSDisk -HostCaching ReadOnly

$vmConfig | Set-AzureDataDisk -LUN 0 -HostCaching ReadWrite
```

```
$vmConfig | Set-AzureDataDisk -LUN 1 -HostCaching ReadWrite

$vmConfig | Update-AzureVM
```

Custom Images, Disks, and Storage Accounts

Before completing this section of the chapter, I want to highlight a few common pitfalls that occur with cloud services, images, disks, and storage accounts.

When creating a virtual machine using your own custom OS image, it is a requirement that the `CurrentStorageAccountName` property of your subscription is set to the same storage account where the image is located. This applies even if they are in the same region. Remember, you set this property by using the `Set-AzureSubscription` cmdlet passing the `-CurrentStorageAccountName` property.

If you do not follow this rule, you will receive the error:

BadRequest: The disk's VHD must be in the same account as the VHD of the source image (source account: storageaccount1.blob.core.windows.net, target account: storageaccount2.blob.core.windows.net).

If you are using a VM image as the source, the behavior is slightly different. Even though the `CurrentStorageAccountName` is not the same location as the VM image location, the cmdlet will succeed. However, the newly created virtual machine's disks will be created in the storage account that the user image is in and not the storage account specified in `CurrentStorageAccountName`.

Another common error that you will receive is when provisioning virtual machines where the image or disk is in one region and the location of the cloud service is in another.

The error for this common problem is as follows:

BadRequest: The location or affinity group North Europe of the storage account where the source image CUSTOMIMAGE resides is not in the same location or affinity group as the specified cloud service. The source image must reside in a storage account that has the same affinity group or location as the cloud service West US.

The resolution to all of these problems is to ensure that all of your assets are in the same location. The cloud service container must always be in the same region as your storage. If you are provisioning from a custom image, the `CurrentStorageAccountName` should match the same region and storage account as your source image.

Managing Storage with PowerShell

You have already seen several of the cmdlets for managing blob storage in Microsoft Azure. While this book is mainly focused on managing infrastructure services, there are some key things to know about managing the underlying system where the virtual machine disks are actually stored.

In addition to the storage account, container, and blob cmdlets, there are also cmdlets that allow you to configure Microsoft Azure storage metrics to monitor storage usage. There are also cmdlets to directly manage tables, queues, and Azure File Services (which is in preview at the time of this writing).

If you would like to see all of the Microsoft Azure storage-related cmdlets, you can use the PowerShell Get-Command cmdlet and filter the Name property for AzureStorage, as shown in Example 5-33.

Example 5-33. Viewing all Microsoft Azure storage cmdlets

```
Get-Command | Where { $_.Name -like "*AzureStorage*" }
```

In the remainder of this chapter I want to focus on some of these cmdlets that specifically impact running and managing virtual machines.

Storage Account Geo-Replication

In Chapter 3 we discussed the basics of creating a Microsoft Azure storage account by using the New-AzureStorageAccount cmdlet. There are some items that merit further review.

Enabling geo-replication on a storage account tells Microsoft Azure to replicate all of the data in the storage account to a remote Microsoft Azure region. Each Microsoft Azure region has a failover region that is used for such purposes. For example, a storage account in the East US region with geo-replication enabled will asynchronously copy all of its data to the West US region.

This is meant to ensure a higher level of durability. Microsoft Azure storage already makes three copies of each blob within the same region. Enabling geo-replication enables an additional three copies of the blob to be replicated to the failover region for additional durability. A storage account with geo-replication enabled gives you six copies of every blob in the storage account. This means there is very little chance that you will have significant data loss due to a failure in the data center.

To enable or disable geo-replication from PowerShell, you can use the Set-AzureStorageAccount cmdlet (see Example 5-34).

Example 5-34. Modifying geo-replication for a storage account

```
Set-AzureStorageAccount -StorageAccountName $storageAccount `
                        -GeoReplicationEnabled $true
```

There are a few reasons why you would want to disable geo-replication on a storage account.

The first should be obvious, and that is cost. Having data stored in multiple regions is going to cost more than storing the data in just a single region. If you are storing non-critical data that does not need the assurance of being replicated to a remote region, then you should disable this option.

The second reason is that not all workloads support geo-replication. For instance, SQL Server does not support having data and transaction logs on separate disks on a geo-replicated storage account. Geo-replication is completely asynchronous. This means that the writes are not guaranteed to be written in order, which makes a transactionally consistent database difficult to restore in the event of a data center failover.

Authenticating Access to Storage

So far, from a security perspective, we have only discussed using the `Select-AzureSubscription` cmdlet and a brief mention of shared access signatures. The `Select-AzureSubscription` cmdlet tells the other cmdlets which subscription to use and, more important, which credentials to use to perform the operation. The current implementation of this approach implies that you are either an administrator or a co-administrator of the Microsoft Azure subscription.

However, there are times when you need to directly authenticate against storage instead of using authentication at the subscription level. A good example is when you need to access a storage account, container, or just a file in a container and you are not an administrator on the Microsoft Azure subscription itself.

There are two methods for authenticating access to storage.

The first method is to use a combination of the storage account name and one of the storage account authentication keys. The second method is generating a shared access signature and passing that to a lower privilege client to use for authentication.

The differences between the two methods is significant. With the storage account name and key, you have full access to everything in the storage account and can perform all operations on its contents. With a shared access signature, the level of access and even the duration of access is defined during the creation of the shared access signature itself. Using a shared access signature is a two-step process. The first step is to generate the SAS token, and this does require full rights on the storage account. The second step is to actually use the SAS token.

Storage context objects

Many of the operations regarding storage accept a storage context parameter. The storage context is simply a data type that stores the authentication method and the credentials used for whatever storage operation you wish to perform. This can either be the storage account name and key or a generated SAS token.

In Example 5-35 I'm using the `Get-AzureStorageKey` cmdlet to retrieve the primary authentication key value and store it in the `$storageKey` variable. I then pass it along with the name of the storage account itself to the `New-AzureStorageContext` cmdlet. This cmdlet creates the context object that can be used by other storage cmdlets to authenticate their operations.

Accessing the storage account key by using the `Get-AzureStorageKey` cmdlet requires Microsoft Azure administrative access. It is possible to retrieve this key as an administrator and pass it to less-elevated code or users. Just remember that whoever has access to the name and key can perform any operation on the contents of the storage account.

Example 5-35. Creating a storage context object using the storage account name and key

```
$storageAccount = "[storage account name]"

$storageKey = (Get-AzureStorageKey -StorageAccountName $storageAccount).Primary

$context = New-AzureStorageContext -StorageAccountName $storageAccount `
                                   -StorageAccountKey $storageKey
```

Passing the `$context` object to the `Get-AzureStorageContainer` cmdlet tells the cmdlet to use the specified storage account and key, whether your local PowerShell configuration has access to the subscription or not (see Example 5-36). You can think of it as an authentication override for storage. If you do not specify a context object to the storage cmdlets, they will assume you want to work on the storage account specified in the `CurrentStorageAccountName` property of your subscription (remember, you can change this setting with the `Set-AzureSubscription` cmdlet).

Example 5-36. Using the context object with Get-AzureStorageBlob

```
$container = "vhds"
Get-AzureStorageBlob -Context $context -Container $container
```

The alternative to passing out the storage account name and key (and full permissions to your storage account) is to generate a shared access signature instead (see Example 5-37). This type of access allows for much finer-grained permissions, duration of permissions, and is also revocable.

To create the shared access signature in the first place, you do need full access to the storage account (see Table 5-6).

Example 5-37. Creating a storage context object using a shared access signature

```
$sas = New-AzureStorageContainerSASToken -Name $container `
                                         -Permission rwdl `
                                         -Context $context
```

Table 5-6. Container permissions for the -Permission parameter

Permission	Symbol	Description
Read	r	Read the content, properties, metadata, or block list of any blob in the container. Use any blob in the container as the source of a copy operation.
Write	w	For any blob in the container, create or write content, properties, metadata, or block list. Snapshot or lease the blob. Resize the blob (page blob only). Use the blob as the destination of a copy operation within the same account.
Delete	d	Delete any blob in the container.
List	l	List blobs in the container.

For more details on blob and container permissions, see the following article in MSDN: *http://bit.ly/shared_access_sig_URI.*

The `New-AzureStorageContainerSASToken` cmdlet creates the actual shared access signature token. You can specify a start time and an end time for how long the token is valid and, optionally, you can specify a previously created Shared Access Signature Policy from which to base the token settings.

Shared access signature policies

At the time of this writing, you can only reference an existing shared access signature policy but you cannot create one using the Power-Shell cmdlets. Of course, you can call .NET, which would allow you to call in the Storage Client Libraries where you have full access to create policies.

When the token has been created, it can be passed to a client and used based on the access that has been granted. To use this token from the Microsoft Azure PowerShell cmdlets, you need to create a storage context object. This time, instead of passing in the the storage account name and key, you will pass in the storage account name and SAS token (see Example 5-38).

When the context object is created, you pass it as a parameter or through the pipeline to any Azure storage cmdlet that accepts a `Context` object as a parameter.

Example 5-38. Using a SAS token from PowerShell

```
$sascontext = New-AzureStorageContext -StorageAccountName $storageAccount `
                         -SasToken $sas


Get-AzureStorageBlob -Context $sascontext -Container $container
```

Setting the Public Access Policy for a Container

The final security topic I want to mention is setting the public access policy for a storage container. Each container within a Microsoft Azure storage account can have an access policy for nonauthenticated (public) requests (see Table 5-7). By default this policy is `Off` on each container but can be changed using the `Set-AzureStorageContainerAcl` cmdlet (see Example 5-39).

Table 5-7. Container access policies

Off	No anonymous access.
Container	Allows read-only access to the blobs in the container and allows the blobs to be enumerated.
Blob	Allows read-only access to the blobs in the container. The requestor needs to know the full path to the blob in question.

Example 5-39. Changing the public access policy of a container

```
$storageAccount = "[storage account name]"

$storageKey = (Get-AzureStorageKey -StorageAccountName $storageAccount).Primary

$context = New-AzureStorageContext -StorageAccountName $storageAccount `
                       -StorageAccountKey $storageKey

# Create a new storage container with Blob public access
New-AzureStorageContainer -Name "newcontainer" -Permission Blob -Context $context

# Modify the container to have the Container public access instead
Set-AzureStorageContainerAcl -Name "newcontainer" `
                       -Permission Container `
                       -Context $context
```

Managing Blob Data

So far I have skirted around managing blob data directly. Let us tackle it head-on in this section.

You have already seen how to create a container by using the New-AzureStorageContainer cmdlet. Let's work off of that knowledge and fill in some of the gaps.

For instance, how do you enumerate all of the existing containers in your storage account? Before creating a new container, how do you test whether the container exists already? How do you delete a container? These are all very good questions that we can quickly address with some examples.

Enumerating containers (see Example 5-40) will show you the current public access policy and the modification date of the container (see Figure 5-16). You can pipe the container output to the `Get-AzureStorageBlob` container and enumerate all of the files in the storage account as well (see Example 5-41 and Figure 5-17).

Example 5-40. Enumerating containers

```
Get-AzureStorageContainer
```

```
PS C:\users\Michael> Get-AzureStorageContainer

   Blob End Point: https://opsgilitytraining.blob.core.windows.net/

Name                          PublicAccess              LastModified
----                          ------------              ------------
opsdemo1                      Off                       2/11/2014 7:15:44 PM +00:00
vhds                          Off                       2/21/2014 2:59:44 PM +00:00
videoexample                  Blob                      2/7/2014 5:36:36 PM +00:00
vmbackup                      Off                       2/20/2014 6:22:01 PM +00:00
```

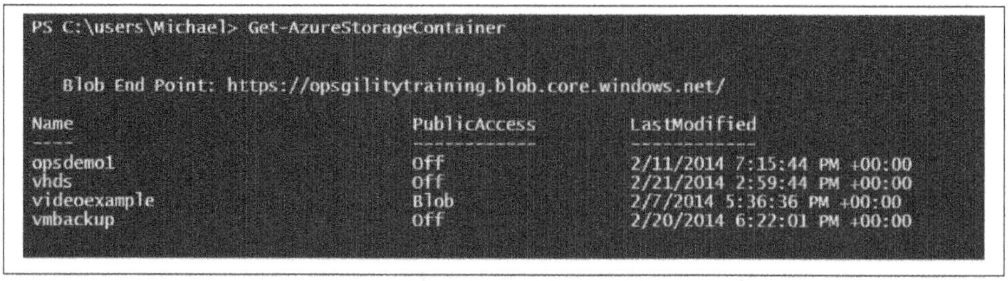

Figure 5-16. Enumerating containers in a storage account

Example 5-41. Enumerating containers and blobs

```
Get-AzureStorageContainer | Get-AzureStorageBlob
```

```
Get-AzureStorageContainer | Get-AzureStorageBlob

   Container Uri: https://opsgilitytraining.blob.core.windows.net/videoexample

Name              BlobType     Length         ContentType      LastModified       SnapshotTime
----              --------     ------         -----------      ------------       ------------
module1-full_...  BlockBlob    1584092622     video/mp4        2/7/2014 5:36...

   Container Uri: https://opsgilitytraining.blob.core.windows.net/vmbackup

Name              BlobType     Length         ContentType      LastModified       SnapshotTime
----              --------     ------         -----------      ------------       ------------
sharepointsub...  PageBlob     136367309312   binary/octet-... 2/20/2014 6:2...
sharepointsub...  PageBlob     21474836992    application/o... 2/20/2014 6:2...
```

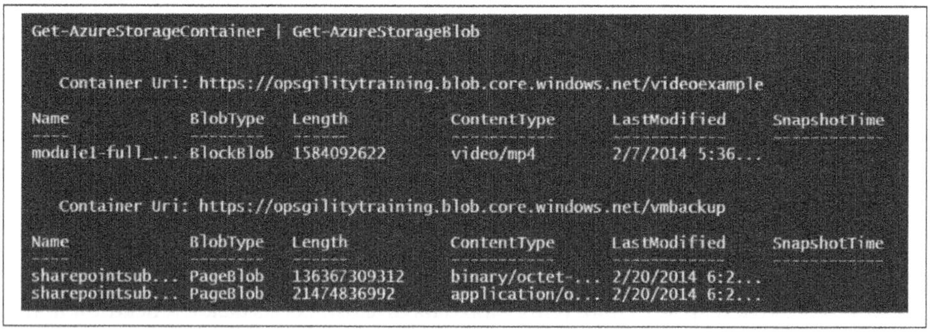

Figure 5-17. Enumerating blobs in a storage account

One of the more useful storage-related tasks is scripting the upload or download of blob data to or from a Microsoft Azure storage account. The cmdlets make this a fairly painless process while at the same time providing you all of the power you would expect as a PowerShell user by supporting the PowerShell pipeline operator. This allows you to enumerate multiple files locally or remotely, and process them as a batch.

You can, of course, take the output of `Get-AzureStorageBlob` and process it via the pipeline too. Passing the output to `Remove-AzureStorageBlob` to delete files or to the `Get-AzureStorageBlobContent` file to download the files locally are two examples of processing you could do with the pipeline output of `Get-AzureStorageBlob`.

In Example 5-42 I am using the Get-AzureStorageContainer output and piping it to Get-AzureStorageBlob. From there, the output is passed to the PowerShell for-each command that allows me to execute a script block for each blob returned. The script block is simple; it creates a local path using the Join-Path cmdlet, the *C:\Temp* directory, and the name of the file (see Figure 5-18).

The returned blob information $_ is piped to the Get-AzureStorageBlobContent cmdlet, which does the heavy lifting of actually downloading the files from the video-example container. Without specifying the videoexample container, this same code could download all of the files in the storage account. It would need a little help to account for creating local folders, but the code change would be minimal.

Example 5-42. Downloading files from a container

```
Get-AzureStorageContainer -Name "videoexample" | Get-AzureStorageBlob | foreach {
    $localPath = Join-Path "C:\Temp" $_.Name
    $_ | Get-AzureStorageBlobContent -Destination $localPath

}
```

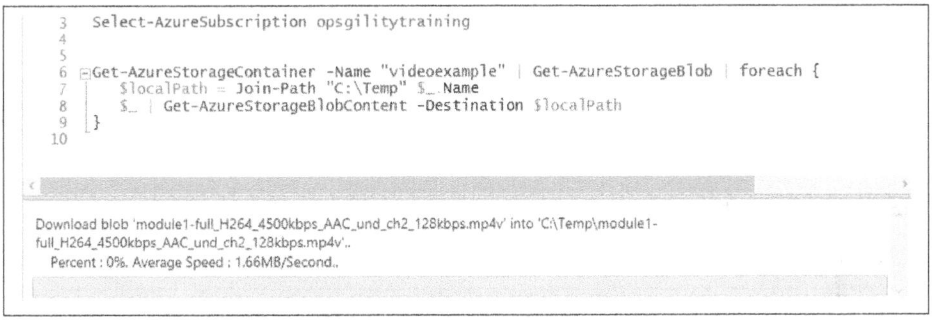

Figure 5-18. Downloading multiple files from storage

Uploading files from the local hard drive to storage is just as simple. In Example 5-43 there are two things going on in order to upload files.

The call to Get-AzureStorageContainer is also passed the -ErrorAction *Silently Continue* in order to test whether the storage container exists or not. If the specified container does not exist, the cmdlet returns $null and the container is created in the New-AzureStorageContainer call.

When the container has been verified to exist, the script uses the Get-ChildItem cmdlet to enumerate all of the files in the *C:\AdventureWorksDB* folder on the C: drive. The path of each file and the name of the container is then passed to the Set-AzureStorageBlobContent cmdlet, which does the heavy lifting of uploading the files. Figure 5-19 shows the upload status using PowerShell ISE.

Example 5-43. Uploading files to a container

```
$localPath = "C:\AdventureWorksDB"
$container = "adventureworks"

$existingContainer = Get-AzureStorageContainer -Name $container `
                                               -ErrorAction SilentlyContinue

If($existingContainer -eq $null)
{
    New-AzureStorageContainer -Name $container
}

Get-ChildItem $localPath | foreach {
    Set-AzureStorageBlobContent -File $_.FullName -Container $container
}
```

```
 2    $localPath = "C:\AdventureWorksDB"
 3    $container = "adventureworks"
 4
 5    $existingContainer = Get-AzureStorageContainer -Name $container `
 6                                                   -ErrorAction SilentlyContinue
 7
 8    If($existingContainer -eq $null)
 9  ⊟{
10         New-AzureStorageContainer -Name $container
11  └}
12
13  ⊟Get-ChildItem $localPath | foreach {
14         Set-AzureStorageBlobContent -File $_.FullName -Container $container
15  └}
```

Upload file 'C:\AdventureWorksDB\AdventureWorks2012_Data.mdf' to blob 'AdventureWorks2012_Data.mdf' in container 'adventureworks'..
Percent : 44%. Average Speed : 1.24MB/Second..

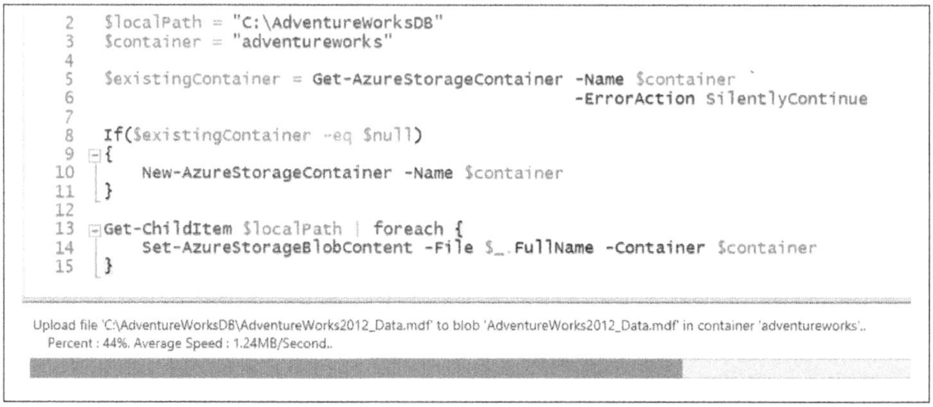

Figure 5-19. Uploading multiple files to storage

Authentication without passing context

You have probably noticed in the previous examples that I have not passed a storage context to any of these calls to storage. When the storage cmdlets are called and the -Context parameter is not specified, the cmdlets will use the currently selected subscription and the CurrentStorageAccountName assocated with it. This property is set by using the Set-AzureSubscription cmdlet.

Asynchronous Blob Copy

The final subject regarding Microsoft Azure storage that I want to cover in this chapter is using the asynchronous blob copy cmdlets. From the perspective of an infrastructure services administrator, this is one of the more critical features of the Microsoft Azure PowerShell cmdlets.

The asynchronous blob copy service allows you to initiate a copy from a source location to a destination location. The beauty is that the source location does not have to be local. You can specify any URL that the copy service itself can access. This could be another Microsoft Azure storage account or just a file on a website. When the copy is initiated, the blob copy service will copy the file from the source to the destination without using your local machine as a middle man.

This opens several scenarios for infrastructure services. You can copy a virtual machine's underlying disks between regions and even between subscriptions. For example, if you have a functioning environment running in the West US region and you would like to copy or move it to East US or even East Asia, you can, all through PowerShell!

Before I dive into the practical aspects of how to do these types of copies in PowerShell, there are some things that you should know about how Azure storage works. For the examples in the table below, I am using four storage accounts.

If I ping each storage account using the full Domain Name System (DNS) name, I can see that opsgilitywest1 and opsgilitywest2 share the same IP address, and that opsgilitywest0 and opsgilityeast1 do not match opsgilitywest1 or opsgilitywest2.

Storage account	FQDN	IP address
opsgilitywest0	opsgilitywest0.blob.core.windows.net	168.62.0.14
opsgilitywest1	opsgilitywest1.blob.core.windows.net	168.63.89.142
opsgilitywest2	opsgilitywest2.blob.core.windows.net	168.63.89.142
opsgilityeast1	opsgilityeast1.blob.core.windows.net	138.91.96.142

Within each Azure region, storage is further subdivided into storage stamps. When you create a storage account, Azure places that storage account in one of the stamps for that region.

How do you know if two storage accounts in the same region are actually in the same stamp? Simply ping the name, and if the IP address returned for each storage account is the same, then they are in the same stamp. In Figure 5-20, the storage accounts opsgilitywest1 and opsgilitywest2 are in the same stamp, but not in the same stamp as opsgilitywest0, even though they are all in the same region.

Storage stamps do not span regions, so opsgilityeast1 is in a completely separate region and stamp than the storage accounts in the West US region (see Figure 5-21).

Why does all of this matter? If you just want to copy files from PowerShell, it shouldn't matter, right? It matters because copying blob data between storage accounts in the same stamp is ridiculously fast when copying files between storage accounts even in the same region, but copying between different stamps is not so fast. Of course, copying files between regions is going to be slowest of all and will vary based on the distance the regions are from each other.

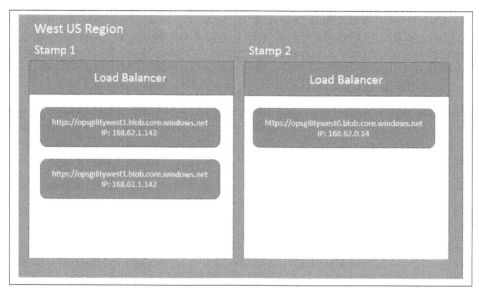

Figure 5-20. Stamps within the same region

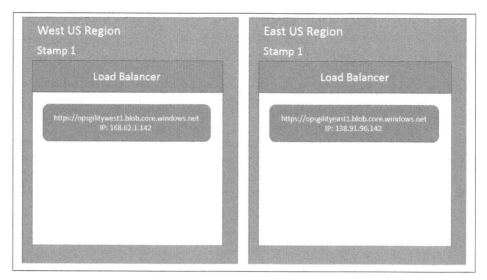

Figure 5-21. Stamps in separate regions

Table 5-8 shows some example copies from testing the copy of a 127 GB OS disk between storage accounts in Microsoft Azure.

Table 5-8. Blob copy time examples

Source	Destination	Result
opsgilitywest1	opsgilitywest1	Shadow Copy—instantaneous
opsgilitywest1	opsgilitywest2	Shadow Copy—instantaneous
opsgilitywest0	opsgilitywest1	Cross-Stamp Copy (12 minutes and 3 seconds)
opsgilitywest1	opsgilityeast1	Cross-Region Copy (22 minutes and 54 seconds)

As you can see, the location of your storage accounts can have a dramatic impact on the performance of a copy operation using the asynchronous blob copy cmdlets. Unfortunately, now that you know this critical information, I do have bad news for you. The bad news is that you cannot directly control the placement of which stamp your storage account will be created in. When you create a new storage account, the stamp is automatically selected for you.

Now that you understand how storage is architected and how the asynchronous blob copy works behind the scenes, let's look at triggering a copy operation between two storage accounts in the same subscription.

Example 5-44 starts by using the `Select-AzureSubscription` cmdlet to set the PowerShell context to the correct subscription. From there it creates a variable `$vhdName` that references the name of the VHD file to copy in the storage account, and the source and destination container names. The next step is to use the `Get-AzureStorageKey` cmdlet to retrieve the primary authentication key for the source and destination storage accounts.

The code then creates two storage context objects for both storage accounts using the `New-AzureStorageContext` cmdlet. This cmdlet is passed the storage account name and key and generates the context object that will be used by the asynchronous blob copy API to authenticate at the source and destination.

The `New-AzureStorageContainer` cmdlet is used with the destination context to create a container on the destination storage account that will hold the copied VHD file.

Finally, the code calls the `Start-AzureStorageBlobCopy` cmdlet, passing the appropriate information for the VHD name on the source and destination, along with the container names and the storage security context objects for both storage accounts.

This cmdlet executes a request to the async blob copy API, and the blob copy state is returned and stored in the `$blobCopyState` variable to use for polling the copy status.

Example 5-44. Copying a VHD in the same subscription between storage accounts

```
# Select the subscription
Select-AzureSubscription "[subscription name]"

$vhdName = "[filename.vhd]"
$srcContainer = "[source container]"
$destContainer = "[destination container]"

# Source storage account
$srcStorage = "[source storage]"

# Destination storage account
$destStorage = "[dest storage]"

$srcStorageKey = (Get-AzureStorageKey -StorageAccountName $srcStorage).Primary

# If the destination storage account is in a separate subscription, switch to the
# destination subscription first to retrieve the storage account key.
# Select-AzureSubscription "[destination subscription name]"

$destStorageKey = (Get-AzureStorageKey -StorageAccountName $destStorage).Primary

# If the destinaton is in a separate subscription,
# switch back to the source subscription here
# Select-AzureSubscription "[subscription name]"


# Create the source storage account context
$srcContext = New-AzureStorageContext   -StorageAccountName $srcStorage `
                                        -StorageAccountKey $srcStorageKey

# Create the destination storage account context
$destContext = New-AzureStorageContext   -StorageAccountName $destStorage `
                                         -StorageAccountKey $destStorageKey

# Create the container on the destination
New-AzureStorageContainer -Name $destContainer -Context $destContext

# Start the asynchronous copy - specify the source authentication with -Context
$blobCopyState = Start-AzureStorageBlobCopy -srcBlob $vhdName `
                                            -srcContainer $srcContainer `
                                            -Context $srcContext `
                                            -DestContainer $destContainer `
                                            -DestBlob $vhdName `
                                            -DestContext $destContext
```

The `Get-AzureStorageBlobCopyState` cmdlet can then be used to validate whether the copy has completed or not. Simply pipe the returned value of a call to `Start-AzureStorageBlobCopy` to the cmdlet, and it will return the current status of the copy operation. You can use this to monitor the status of the async copy to know when it is complete (see Example 5-45).

Example 5-45. Monitoring the copy status

```
# Retrieve the current status of the copy operation
$status = $blobCopyState | Get-AzureStorageBlobCopyState

# Print out status
$status

# Loop until complete
While($status.Status -eq "Pending"){
  $status = $blobCopyState | Get-AzureStorageBlobCopyState
  Start-Sleep 10
  # Print out status
  $status
}
```

Example 5-46 is a working example with values from my subscription added to show a practical aspect to the sample.

Example 5-46. Full blob copy example

```
# Select the subscription
Select-AzureSubscription "opsgilitytraining"

# Retrieved the OS disk name using:
# Get-AzureVM -ServiceName "psdeploysvc" -Name "psdeploy" | Get-AzureOSDisk
$vhdName = "psdeploysvc-psdeploy-2014-03-17.vhd"
$srcContainer = "vhds"
$destContainer = "copiedvhds"

# Source storage account
$srcStorage = "opsgilitywest"

# Destination storage account
$destStorage = "opsgilityeast1"

$srcStorageKey = (Get-AzureStorageKey -StorageAccountName $srcStorage).Primary


$destStorageKey = (Get-AzureStorageKey -StorageAccountName $destStorage).Primary

# Create the source storage account context
$srcContext = New-AzureStorageContext  -StorageAccountName $srcStorage `
                                -StorageAccountKey $srcStorageKey

# Create the destination storage account context
$destContext = New-AzureStorageContext  -StorageAccountName $destStorage `
                                -StorageAccountKey $destStorageKey

# Create the container on the destination
```

```
New-AzureStorageContainer -Name $destContainer -Context $destContext

# Start the asynchronous copy - specify the source authentication with -Context
$blobCopyState = Start-AzureStorageBlobCopy -srcBlob $vhdName `
                                            -srcContainer $srcContainer `
                                            -Context $srcContext `
                                            -DestContainer $destContainer `
                                            -DestBlob $vhdName `
                                            -DestContext $destContext

# Retrieve the current status of the copy operation
$status = $blobCopyState | Get-AzureStorageBlobCopyState

# Print out status
$status

# Loop until complete
While($status.Status -eq "Pending"){
  $status = $blobCopyState | Get-AzureStorageBlobCopyState
  Start-Sleep 10
  # Print out status
  $status
}
```

To retrieve the OS disk name, I piped the results of Get-AzureVM to the Get-AzureOSDisk cmdlet to extract the OS disk information (see Figure 5-22).

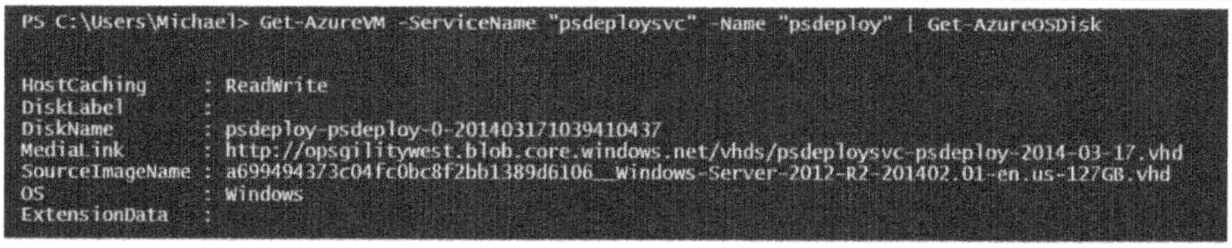

Figure 5-22. Viewing the OS disk name with Get-AzureOSDisk

The storage accounts are in separate regions, so the copy operation takes anywhere from 7 to 12 minutes. The simple loop at the end of the script will print out the status of the copy operation every 10 seconds, updating the progress (see Figure 5-23).

Summary

In this chapter, we explored Microsoft Azure storage in the context of Microsoft Azure Virtual Machines. While this chapter is not comprehensive, I do hope it helps you understand the capabilities of the platform and hits on the key tasks that a Microsoft Azure administrator will likely be given with automating. In the next chapter we will discuss automation with Microsoft Azure Virtual Networks, including features such as the internal load balancer, and hybrid technologies such as site-to-site, point-to-site, and ExpressRoute.

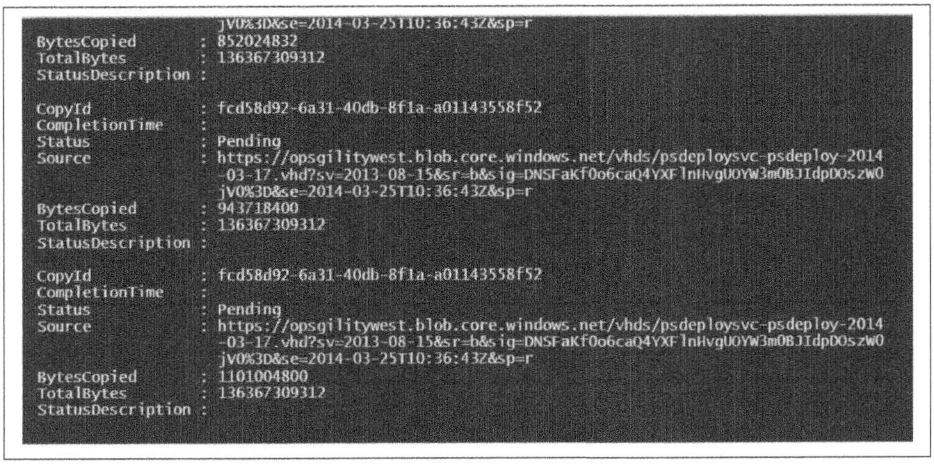

```
                        jV0%3D&se=2014-03-25T10:36:43Z&sp=r
BytesCopied        : 852024832
TotalBytes         : 136367309312
StatusDescription  :

CopyId             : fcd58d92-6a31-40db-8f1a-a01143558f52
CompletionTime     :
Status             : Pending
Source             : https://opsgilitywest.blob.core.windows.net/vhds/psdeploysvc-psdeploy-2014
                     -03-17.vhd?sv=2013-08-15&sr=b&sig=DNSFaKf0o6caQ4YXFlnHvgUOYW3mOBJIdpDOszW0
                     jV0%3D&se=2014-03-25T10:36:43Z&sp=r
BytesCopied        : 943718400
TotalBytes         : 136367309312
StatusDescription  :

CopyId             : fcd58d92-6a31-40db-8f1a-a01143558f52
CompletionTime     :
Status             : Pending
Source             : https://opsgilitywest.blob.core.windows.net/vhds/psdeploysvc-psdeploy-2014
                     -03-17.vhd?sv=2013-08-15&sr=b&sig=DNSFaKf0o6caQ4YXFlnHvgUOYW3mOBJIdpDOszW0
                     jV0%3D&se=2014-03-25T10:36:43Z&sp=r
BytesCopied        : 1101004800
TotalBytes         : 136367309312
StatusDescription  :
```

Figure 5-23. Checking the blob copy state

## CHAPTER 6

Virtual Networks

Microsoft Azure Virtual Networks are a critical feature for many scenarios. Deploying a virtual machine into a virtual network allows several key features that may be required with more-advanced virtual machine workloads. The ability to specify static IP addresses, Domain Name System (DNS) servers, and internal load balancing; and to enable hybrid connectivity to an on-premises data center, or even secure access from an individual client machine, are all possible with virtual networks.

Virtual networks also provide the ability to connect virtual machines in other cloud services and even other virtual networks to create a larger isolated network. This private network can potentially span multiple Microsoft Azure regions globally and even multiple on-premises sites.

Virtual networks allow you to control name resolution as well. You can define one or more DNS servers to assign to the virtual machines that are deployed into the virtual network. This allows workloads such as Active Directory or any other scenario where you need automatic DNS server assignment.

Now that you know a little about why virtual networks are so useful and powerful, let's dive in and see how we can use PowerShell to manage them.

Understanding Virtual Network Configuration

The support for creating and updating virtual networks directly from PowerShell is relatively primitive. There are two key cmdlets that can assist: `Get-AzureVNetConfig` and `Set-AzureVNetConfig`. Each cmdlet works by either returning an XML file or by passing an XML file.

Unfortunately, there are no convenience cmdlets for abstracting away the XML (like `Add-AzureVirtualNetwork` or `Add-AzureSubnet`). During the initial development, these cmdlets were in scope; but like all projects, features had to be cut to ship on time and those additional cmdlets just have not been added back since.

So now that you know that there are no convenience cmdlets to create and update virtual networks, how can you accomplish the task via PowerShell? The answer is to use PowerShell's native support for XML to add or remove settings in your subscription's virtual network configuration in combination with the `Get-AzureVNetConfig` and `Set-AzureVNetConfig` cmdlets to specify your subscription's current network configuration.

For example, to retrieve the XML configuration for your current subscription, you can use the `Get-AzureVNetConfig` cmdlet. There are two methods for retrieving the network configuration with `Get-AzureVNetConfig`. The first is to simply save it to a local path for viewing or manipulation. This is equivalent to using the management portal to export your network configuration to disk (see Example 6-1).

Example 6-1. Exporting network configuration

```
Get-AzureVNetConfig -ExportToFile "C:\Users\Michael\NetworkConfiguration.xml"
```

The second method can be used to store the XML configuration within a variable. This is useful if you need to manipulate or read the configuration from your script (see Example 6-2).

Example 6-2. Storing the returned data in an XML variable

```
$networkConfiguration = [xml] (Get-AzureVNetConfig).XMLConfiguration
```

If there is no configuration at all, the data returned will be `$null`. If the return value is `$null`, you can set the configuration to whatever valid network configuration you think the subscription should have by using the `Set-AzureVNetConfig` cmdlet. This is equivalent to using the management portal to import an existing network configuration XML file (see Example 6-3).

Example 6-3. Importing a network configuration

```
Set-AzureVNetConfig -ConfigurationPath "C:\Users\Michael\NewNetworkConfiguration.xml"
```

It is important to understand how virtual networks are created, updated, or deleted in order to do this correctly. The underlying API to modify your virtual network configuration requires that the network configuration for your entire subscription is passed with each update.

What this means to you as someone designing automation is that you first need to retrieve the current virtual network configuration (XML), if it is not $null, then modify the XML by adding, updating, or deleting whatever configuration needs to be changed. When the XML has been modified, send the changed configuration back by using the `Set-AzureVnetConfig` cmdlet.

Dynamically Adding a Virtual Network

In this section of the chapter we will walk through a simplified but realistic example of using PowerShell to dynamically add a virtual network to a Microsoft Azure subscription. The example will take an existing network configuration file (XML) that contains a very simple virtual network and add it to the networking configuration of a Microsoft Azure subscription.

To build this script on your own, I would recommend creating a new PowerShell file and saving it with a name such as *chapter6addvnet.ps1*.

In the same directory as your script, create a new text file and change the name to *NewVNETConfig.xml*. Once created, add the contents shown in Example 6-4 to the file and save it.

Example 6-4. Network configuration (NewVNETConfig.xml)

```xml
<?xml version="1.0" encoding="utf-8"?>
<NetworkConfiguration xmlns:xsd="http://www.w3.org/2001/XMLSchema"
xmlns:xsi="http://www.w3.org/2001/XMLSchema-instance"
xmlns="http://schemas.microsoft.com/ServiceHosting/2011/07/NetworkConfiguration">

  <VirtualNetworkConfiguration>
    <VirtualNetworkSites>
        <VirtualNetworkSite name="PSBookVNET" Location="[region name]">
            <AddressSpace>
                <AddressPrefix>10.20.0.0/16</AddressPrefix>
            </AddressSpace>
            <Subnets>
                <Subnet name="AppSubnet">
                <AddressPrefix>10.20.1.0/24</AddressPrefix>
                </Subnet>
                <Subnet name="DCSubnet">
                <AddressPrefix>10.20.2.0/24</AddressPrefix>
                </Subnet>
            </Subnets>
        </VirtualNetworkSite>
    </VirtualNetworkSites>
  </VirtualNetworkConfiguration>
</NetworkConfiguration>
```

Replace the *[region name]* placeholder with the region in which you want to create the virtual network. Remember, you can identify all of the regions available for your subscription with the Get-AzureLocation cmdlet.

The *NewVNETConfig.xml* file contains a complete network configuration for a Microsoft Azure subscription. However, if an existing configuration is already in place, you will need to merge the contents of the XML file with the existing configuration.

In this specific example, the only element we are interested in merging is the `<Virtual NetworkSite>`. This element describes a very simple but functionally complete virtual network with two subnets. In more-realistic scenarios you will deal with many other configuration elements such as `DNS`, `LocalNetworkSites`, and `Gateways`. For a complete review of the Microsoft Azure Virtual Network schema, consult the authoritative source at MSDN (*http://bit.ly/VirtualNetworkConfiguration*).

The first set of code to add to the *chapter6addvnet.ps1* script is to define the variables for the script. These are the Microsoft Azure subscription name and the path to the XML file that contains the new virtual network to import (see Example 6-5).

Example 6-5. Creating the parameters (Script pane)

```
[CmdletBinding()]
param(
[parameter(Mandatory)]
[string]$subscription,
[parameter(Mandatory)]
[string]$newVNetConfigPath
)
```

The next step is to call the `Select-AzureSubscription` cmdlet to specify the subscription in which the virtual network will be created. The script then loads the XML file containing the new virtual network and extracts the virtual network name by using PowerShell's native XML handing capabilities (see Example 6-6).

Example 6-6. Loading the virtual network configuration (Script pane)

```
Select-AzureSubscription $subscription

[xml] $nxml =  Get-Content $newVNetConfigPath

[Xml.XmlElement]$nVNet = $nxml.NetworkConfiguration.VirtualNetworkConfiguration

# New VNET name
$nvname = $nVNet.VirtualNetworkSites.VirtualNetworkSite.name
```

The next step is to return the existing virtual network configuration from the Microsoft Azure subscription. This step is performed using the `Get-AzureVNetConfig` cmdlet.

The return value of this cmdlet contains the `XMLConfiguration` property, which can be cast using the `[xml]` qualifier and stored in a variable for manipulation (see Example 6-7). The return value can also be `$null`, which means that the subscription has no current network configuration. In the event that the subscription does not have a network configuration, the script simply calls the `Set-AzureVNetConfig` cmdlet and specifies the XML configuration file. If this branch of the script is followed, the contents of this file will become the network configuration for the subscription.

Example 6-7. Retrieving and verifying the existing network configuration (Script pane)

```
# Retrieve the current subscription network configuration
$exml = [xml] (Get-AzureVNetConfig).XMLConfiguration


if($exml -eq $null)
{
    Write-Output "Existing network configuration not found."
    Write-Output "Applying entire configuration."
    Set-AzureVNetConfig -ConfigurationPath $newVNetConfigPath
    return
}
```

The next portion of the script assumes there is an existing network configuration to deal with. In this case the script will perform some basic validation to ensure that there are no existing virtual networks with the same name; if there is, the script will exit (see Example 6-8). A more advanced automation script could attempt to merge any updated properties such as DNS, Subnets, and so on that differ between the virtual networks.

Example 6-8. Testing for an existing virtual network with the same name (Script pane)

```
# Existing virtual networks

[Xml.XmlElement]$eVNet = $exml.NetworkConfiguration.VirtualNetworkConfiguration

$esite = $eVNet.VirtualNetworkSites.VirtualNetworkSite

if($esite -ne $null)
{
    foreach($vnet in $esite)
    {
        if($vnet.Name -eq $nvname)
        {
            Write-Output "$nvname already exists - exiting."
            return
        }
    }
}
```

The final portion of the script uses PowerShell's XML processing capabilities of merging the new VirtualNetworkSite element from the passed-in XML configuration retrieved from the Microsoft Azure subscription. When the XML is merged, a new XML file is created in a temporary location on the filesystem and is then passed to the Set-AzureVNetConfig cmdlet. The final step is to remove the newly created temporary XML file by using the Remove-Item cmdlet (see Examples 6-9 and 6-10).

Example 6-9. Merging the new virtual network with the existing configuration (Script pane)

```
$newSite = $nVNet.VirtualNetworkSites.VirtualNetworkSite

$importedVnet = $exml.ImportNode($newSite, $true)

$eVNet.VirtualNetworkSites.AppendChild($importedVnet)

$tmpFile = Join-Path $env:TEMP "NewNetConfig.xml"

$exml.Save($tmpFile)

Write-Output "Importing new virtual network to existing network configuration"
Set-AzureVNetConfig -ConfigurationPath $tmpFile

# Delete the temporary file
Remove-Item $tmpFile
```

Example 6-10. Complete example

```
[CmdletBinding()]
param(
[parameter(Mandatory)]
[string]$subscription,
[parameter(Mandatory)]
[string]$newVNetConfigPath
)

Select-AzureSubscription $subscription

[xml] $nxml =  Get-Content $newVNetConfigPath

[Xml.XmlElement]$nVNet = $nxml.NetworkConfiguration.VirtualNetworkConfiguration


# New VNET name
$nvname = $nVNet.VirtualNetworkSites.VirtualNetworkSite.name

# Retrieve the current subscription network configuration
$exml = [xml] (Get-AzureVNetConfig).XMLConfiguration


if($econfig -eq $null)
{
    Write-Output "Existing network configuration not found."
    Write-Output "Applying entire configuration."
    Set-AzureVNetConfig -ConfigurationPath $newVNetConfigPath
    return
}

# Existing virtual networks
```

```
[Xml.XmlElement]$eVNet = $exml.NetworkConfiguration.VirtualNetworkConfiguration

$esite = $eVNet.VirtualNetworkSites.VirtualNetworkSite

if($esite -ne $null)
{
    foreach($vnet in $esite)
    {
        if($vnet.Name -eq $nvname)
        {
            Write-Output "$nvname already exists - exiting."
            return
        }
    }
}

$newSite = $nVNet.VirtualNetworkSites.VirtualNetworkSite

$importedVnet = $exml.ImportNode($newSite, $true)

$eVNet.VirtualNetworkSites.AppendChild($importedVnet)

$tmpFile = Join-Path $env:TEMP "NewNetConfig.xml"

$exml.Save($tmpFile)

Write-Output "Importing new virtual network to existing network configuration"
Set-AzureVNetConfig -ConfigurationPath $tmpFile

# Delete the temporary file
Remove-Item $tmpFile
```

When you have completed writing the script, the last step is to execute it by pressing F5, or by highlighting the script and pressing F8. You will be prompted for the variables defined at the beginning of the script (see Figure 6-1). Enter the subscription name and the path to the *NewVNETConfig.xml* file (quotes around the values are not needed even if there are spaces in the subscription name or path to the XML file).

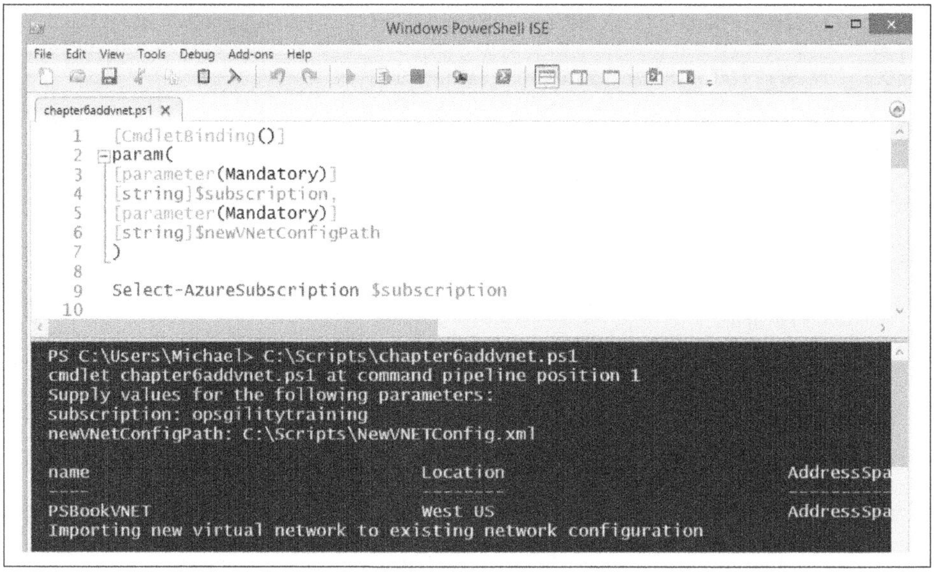

```
                              Windows PowerShell ISE                    - □ ×
File  Edit  View  Tools  Debug  Add-ons  Help
  □ ☞ 🖫 ℓ ᘐ □ ⋋  ᔭ ℃  ▶ ⓑ ▦  ⬚ ⬚  ▤ ☐ □  ⬚ ☐ ⸱
┌ chapter6addvnet.ps1 X ┐                                                  ⌃
    1     [CmdletBinding()]                                                ⌃
    2   ⊟param(
    3     [parameter(Mandatory)]
    4     [string]$subscription,
    5     [parameter(Mandatory)]
    6     [string]$newVNetConfigPath
    7   └)
    8
    9     Select-AzureSubscription $subscription
   10                                                                      ⌄
  <                                                                      >

 PS C:\Users\Michael> C:\Scripts\chapter6addvnet.ps1                       ⌃
 cmdlet chapter6addvnet.ps1 at command pipeline position 1
 Supply values for the following parameters:
 subscription: opsgilitytraining
 newVNetConfigPath: C:\Scripts\NewVNETConfig.xml

 name                          Location                    AddressSpa
 --------                      --------                    ----------
 PSBookVNET                    West US                     AddressSpa
 Importing new virtual network to existing network configuration
```

Figure 6-1. Add virtual network by using Set-AzureVNetConfig

Real-world validation

Like most examples in this book, this example does not validate for
all failure cases. In the previous example, if you wish to validate the
configuration before executing, there are several items to check.
First, you could validate the incoming XML file against the virtual
network schema. Second, you could validate the subscription quo-
tas to ensure that you can actually allocate another virtual network
in the subscription. Finally, you could also check that the region
specified in the virtual network is valid within the subscription you
are using by comparing it against the available names returned from
the Get-AzureLocation cmdlet.

Updating a Virtual Network Configuration

The experience of updating an existing virtual network is almost identical to creating a
new one. You first retrieve the configuration by using Get-AzureVNetConfig, modify
the XML, and send the modified changes back to the subscription with a call to Set-
AzureVNetConfig.

Deleting a virtual network

Deleting a virtual network consists of removing it from the network configuration XML
file and sending the new configuration (minus the virtual network) back with

`Set-AzureVNetConfig`. One thing to remember is you cannot delete a virtual network that has a gateway, virtual machines, or cloud service instances provisioned into the virtual network. When these compute resources are deleted, you can delete the virtual network.

Adding or removing DNS

You can add DNS servers to your virtual network configuration by modifying the XML configuration to match the schema outlined in MSDN. Similar to deleting a virtual network, you cannot remove a DNS server from a virtual network if any compute resources are provisioned into the virtual network that is referencing the DNS server. You can add new DNS servers to the virtual network, but existing virtual machines must be rebooted to see the new DNS server.

Adding or removing subnets and local network sites

Similar to DNS, you can add or remove subnets or a local network site configuration by modifying the XML configuration. You must first remove any virtual machines or cloud service instances assigned to a subnet before deleting it.

Removing the Network Configuration

I also want to mention the `Remove-AzureVnetConfig` cmdlet. This cmdlet is very handy for clearing all of your virtual network settings from a subscription. The only time you can execute this cmdlet is when you have no virtual machine or cloud service instances provisioned in any virtual network in your subscription.

The syntax for executing the cmdlet is straightforward; see Example 6-11.

Example 6-11. Removing an existing virtual network configuration

```
Remove-AzureVNetConfig
```

Now that you know the basics of constructing or updating the virtual network schema, let's discuss how to provision a virtual machine into the virtual network we just created.

Provisioning into a Virtual Network

The `New-AzureVM` and `New-AzureQuickVM` cmdlets support specifying a `VNetName` as a parameter to deploy a virtual machine into a virtual network. In the following pages we will write examples to show how with each cmdlet.

To get started, you will need the details of your current network configuration. To accomplish this, `Get-AzureVNetConfig` can be used along with the `select` command and

`-ExpandProperty` parameter to expand the `XMLConfiguration` element of the returned configuration (see Example 6-12 and Figure 6-2).

Example 6-12. Using Get-AzureVNETConfig to display the virtual network configuration (Console pane)

```
Get-AzureVNetConfig | select -ExpandProperty XMLConfiguration
```

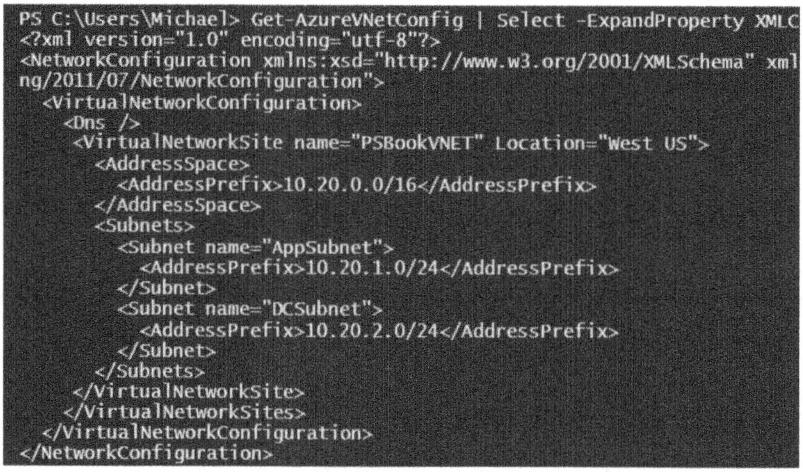

```
PS C:\Users\Michael> Get-AzureVNetConfig | Select -ExpandProperty XMLC
<?xml version="1.0" encoding="utf-8"?>
<NetworkConfiguration xmlns:xsd="http://www.w3.org/2001/XMLSchema" xml
ng/2011/07/NetworkConfiguration">
  <VirtualNetworkConfiguration>
    <Dns />
    <VirtualNetworkSite name="PSBookVNET" Location="West US">
      <AddressSpace>
        <AddressPrefix>10.20.0.0/16</AddressPrefix>
      </AddressSpace>
      <Subnets>
        <Subnet name="AppSubnet">
          <AddressPrefix>10.20.1.0/24</AddressPrefix>
        </Subnet>
        <Subnet name="DCSubnet">
          <AddressPrefix>10.20.2.0/24</AddressPrefix>
        </Subnet>
      </Subnets>
    </VirtualNetworkSite>
  </VirtualNetworkSites>
  </VirtualNetworkConfiguration>
</NetworkConfiguration>
```

Figure 6-2. Get-AzureVNETConfig output

The first example we will write is to use `New-AzureQuickVM` to provision into a virtual network. Using the PowerShell ISE, create a new file called *chapter6quickvmvnet.ps1* and add the source shown in Example 6-13, ensuring that you replace the placeholder values with real values. For this example you should use a new cloud service name.

Example 6-13. Using the New-AzureQuickVM cmdlet to join a virtual network and specify a subnet (Script pane)

```
# Specify the admin credentials
$adminUser = "[admin username]"
$password = "[admin password]"

$serviceName = "[cloud service name]"
$VNET = "PSBookVNET"
$Location = "West US"
$Subnet = "AppSubnet"

$vmName = "vnetjoinedvm1"
$vmSize = "Small"

$imageFamily = "Windows Server 2012 R2 Datacenter"
```

```
$imageName = Get-AzureVMImage |
                where { $_.ImageFamily -eq $imageFamily } |
                sort PublishedDate -Descending |
                select -ExpandProperty ImageName -First 1

New-AzureQuickVM -Windows `
                -ServiceName $serviceName `
                -Name $vmName `
                -InstanceSize $vmSize `
                -ImageName $imageName `
                -Location $location `
                -AdminUsername $adminUser `
                -Password $password `
                -VNetName $VNET `
                -SubnetNames $Subnet
```

The -SubnetNames parameter accepts an array of subnets, but it is actually not doing what you may think. Currently, virtual machines in Microsoft Azure support only a single network interface, so your virtual machine will be deployed on only a single subnet. So why have more than one? Simple: if the address space on the first subnet is full (no more available IP addresses), Microsoft Azure will allocate an IP from one of the additional subnets if they are specified.

Execute the script by pressing F5, or by highlighting the script and pressing F8, to create the first virtual machine in your virtual network.

The second example shows how to provision a virtual machine by using the composition model with the New-AzureVMConfig and New-AzureVM cmdlets. Using the PowerShell ISE, create a new PowerShell file called *chapter6createvmvnet.ps1* and add the source shown in Example 6-14. As always, ensure that you replace the placeholder values with real values. For this example you should also use a new cloud service name.

Example 6-14. Joining a virtual network by using the virtual machine composition model (Script pane)

```
# Specify the admin credentials
$adminUser = "[admin username]"
$password = "[admin password]"
$serviceName = "[cloud service name]"

$VNET = "PSBookVNET"
$Location = "West US"
$Subnet = "AppSubnet"

$vmName = "vnetjoinedvm2"
$vmSize = "Small"

$imageFamily = "Windows Server 2012 R2 Datacenter"

$imageName = Get-AzureVMImage |
```

```
                where { $_.ImageFamily -eq $imageFamily } |
                sort PublishedDate -Descending |
                select -ExpandProperty ImageName -First 1

$vmConfig = New-AzureVMConfig -Name $vmName `
                            -InstanceSize $vmSize `
                            -ImageName $imageName

$vmConfig | Add-AzureProvisioningConfig -Windows -AdminUsername $adminUser `
                            -Password $password

$vmConfig | Set-AzureSubnet -SubnetNames $Subnet

$vmConfig | New-AzureVM -ServiceName $serviceName -Location $location -VNetName $VNET
```

Only minor changes were made to the previous composition example to demonstrate how to join a virtual network. The first change is the introduction of a new cmdlet, Set-AzureSubnet. This cmdlet takes the virtual machine configuration and modifies it by setting the SubnetNames property. The second change is the addition of the VNetName parameter on the New-AzureVM cmdlet call.

Execute the script by pressing F5, or by highlighting the script and pressing F8, to create the second virtual machine in your virtual network.

Cross-service connectivity

If you have executed the previous two examples, you should have two virtual machines in separate cloud services on the same virtual network. To demonstrate that the virtual machines can communicate directly even though they are in separate cloud services, log in to vnetjoinedvm1 using remote desktop and from within that virtual machine log in to vnetjoinedvm2 using its internal IP address.

Understanding IP Address Assignment

When a virtual machine is deployed into a virtual network, its internal IP address is assigned from the subnet specified in Set-AzureSubnet and is dependent on the order in which it was provisioned (unless a static IP is specified, which will be discussed soon).

For example, the AppSubnet subnet created in the previous example uses the address prefix of 10.20.1.0/24. The first four IP addresses of each subnet are reserved. With this knowledge in hand, it is easy to deduce that the first IP address available in this subnet will be 10.20.1.4. Unless otherwise specified, a virtual machine will be assigned the next available IP address from the subnet to which it was assigned at provisioning time.

The IP address assigned to each virtual machine will not change unless the virtual machine is deallocated. How do you deallocate a virtual machine? Simply use the

Stop-AzureVM cmdlet (without using the -StayProvisioned parameter) or shut down from within the management portal. If the status of your virtual machine is StoppedDeallocated, then the virtual machine is no longer allocated and you are not being billed for the compute time. You should remember that shutting down your virtual machine from within the virtual machine itself does not deallocate the virtual machine and it will retain its IP address (and bill you while shut down).

To further illustrate the IP addressing scheme that Microsoft Azure uses, let's walk through the IP address assignments for four virtual machines in the same subnet range of 10.20.1.0/24, shown in Example 6-15.

If you would like to try this experiment out on your own, you should first delete any virtual machines you may have created in the PSBookVNET virtual network. Then, using your PowerShell ISE, create a new PowerShell script named *chapter6createvmsvnet.ps1*.

Example 6-15. Creating multiple virtual machines (Script pane)

```
# Replace with your own subscription name
Select-AzureSubscription "[subscription name]"

# Specify the admin credentials
$adminUser = "[admin username]"
$password = "[admin password]"


# Replace with your cloud service name
$serviceName = "[cloud service name]"

$VNET = "PSBookVNET"
$Location = "West US"
$Subnet = "AppSubnet"

$vmSize = "Small"
$imageFamily = "Windows Server 2012 R2 Datacenter"

$imageName = Get-AzureVMImage |
             where { $_.ImageFamily -eq $imageFamily } |
             sort PublishedDate -Descending |
             select -ExpandProperty ImageName -First 1


$vmConfigs = @()

for($i=1; $i -le 4; $i++)
{
    # Change the VM name to match the instance number
    $vmName = "vnetjoinedvm$i"

    $vmConfig = New-AzureVMConfig -Name $vmName `
                                  -InstanceSize $vmSize `
```

```
                              -ImageName $imageName

    $vmConfig | Add-AzureProvisioningConfig -Windows `
                                            -AdminUsername $adminUser `
                                            -Password $password

    $vmConfig | Set-AzureSubnet -SubnetNames $Subnet

    $vmConfigs += $vmConfig
}

# Create the virtual machines by passing an array of configurations
# New-AzureVM will create them on your behalf in the same cloud service
New-AzureVM -ServiceName $serviceName `
            -Location $Location `
            -VNetName $VNET `
            -VMs $vmConfigs
```

To view the internal IP addresses assigned to each virtual machine, you can use the Get-AzureVM cmdlet and select the virtual machine name and the IP address (see Example 6-16 and Figure 6-3).

Example 6-16. Viewing internal IP addresses for your virtual machines (Console pane)

```
Get-AzureVM -ServiceName $serviceName | select Name, IpAddress
```

```
PS C:\Users\Michael> get-azurevm -ServiceName $serviceName | select Name, IpAddress

Name                                                IpAddress
----                                                ---------
vnetjoinedvm1                                       10.20.1.4
vnetjoinedvm2                                       10.20.1.5
vnetjoinedvm3                                       10.20.1.6
vnetjoinedvm4                                       10.20.1.7
```

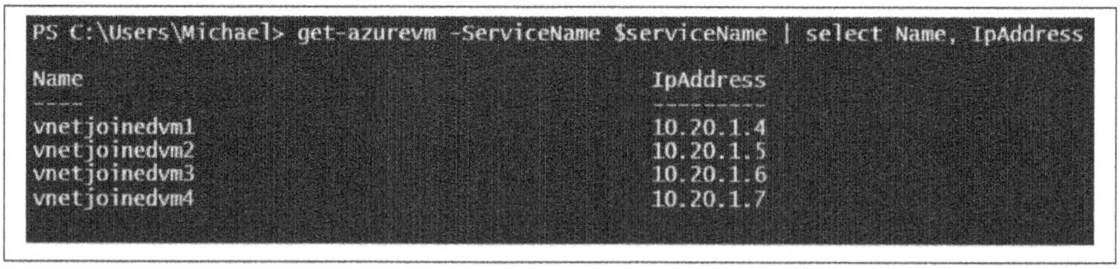

Figure 6-3. Name and IP address assignment at creation

If all of the virtual machines are shut down using Stop-AzureVM and then started in a different order, the IP addresses will be assigned in the order they were started (see Example 6-17 and the resulting assignments in Figure 6-4).

Example 6-17. Shut down and started out of order (Console pane)

```
# Replace with your cloud service name
$serviceName = "[cloud service name]"

# Stop all virtual machines in the cloud service
Get-AzureVM -ServiceName $serviceName | Stop-AzureVM -Force


Start-AzureVM -ServiceName $serviceName -Name "vnetjoinedvm4"
```

```
Start-AzureVM -ServiceName $serviceName -Name "vnetjoinedvm1"
Start-AzureVM -ServiceName $serviceName -Name "vnetjoinedvm2"
Start-AzureVM -ServiceName $serviceName -Name "vnetjoinedvm3"
```

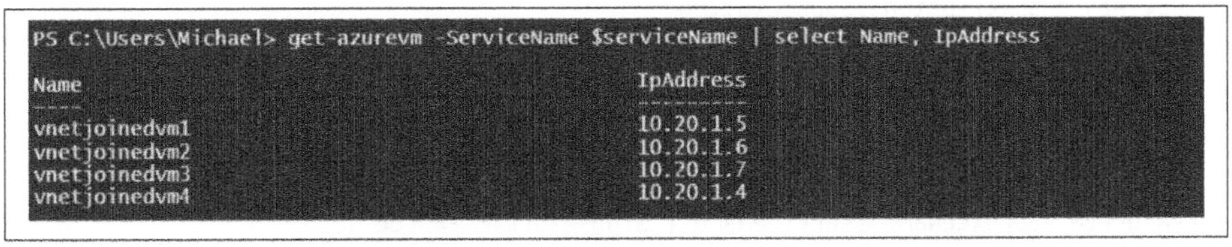

```
PS C:\Users\Michael> get-azurevm -ServiceName $serviceName | select Name, IpAddress

Name                                        IpAddress
----                                        ---------
vnetjoinedvm1                               10.20.1.5
vnetjoinedvm2                               10.20.1.6
vnetjoinedvm3                               10.20.1.7
vnetjoinedvm4                               10.20.1.4
```

Figure 6-4. Name and IP address assignment with modified start order

Specifying Static IP Addresses

Having the IP addresses of your virtual machines depend on the start order may or may not be acceptable in your situation. In some workloads, such as DNS servers, if the IP address changes, the result could be catastrophic to your deployment.

The first solution you might think of is to just not shut down those virtual machines. However, that removes one of the key benefits of the cloud in the first place: pay-as-you-go computing. If you do not need your servers running for whatever reason, you should not be required to. It is also risky because with multiple administrators (or sometimes even just one) accidents will happen.

A better solution is to use *static IP addresses*. Static IP addresses allow you to request a specific IP address be assigned to a virtual machine when it starts. One thing to note is this is a request and not a reservation. If another virtual machine already has the static IP address assigned to it (and yes, it is available for automatic assignment), when your virtual machine is started, it will fail to boot. You can mitigate this risk by deploying all virtual machines with static IP addresses into a separate subnet.

Example 6-18 first shuts down all of the existing virtual machines so their IP addresses are free for assignment. It then updates the virtual machines by retrieving their current configuration with `Get-AzureVM`, modifies that configuration by using `Set-AzureStaticVNetIP`, and sends the updated configuration to Azure with `Update-AzureVM`.

When the virtual machines have static IP addresses assigned, `Start-AzureVM` is called for each of them in the same order as before, and, as Figure 6-5 shows, the virtual machines have the expected IP addresses.

To try this on your own, create a new PowerShell script named *chapter6setstatic.ps1* and add the code in Example 6-18.

Example 6-18. Specifying static IP addresses (Script pane)

```
# Replace with your own subscription name
$subscription = "[subscription name]"

Select-AzureSubscription $subscription

# Replace with your cloud service name
$serviceName = "[cloud service name]"

# Stop all virtual machines in the cloud service
Get-AzureVM -ServiceName $serviceName | Stop-AzureVM -Force


Get-AzureVM -ServiceName $serviceName -Name vnetjoinedvm1 |
    Set-AzureStaticVNetIP -IPAddress "10.20.1.4" |
    Update-AzureVM

Get-AzureVM -ServiceName $serviceName -Name vnetjoinedvm2 |
    Set-AzureStaticVNetIP -IPAddress "10.20.1.5" |
    Update-AzureVM

Get-AzureVM -ServiceName $serviceName -Name vnetjoinedvm3 |
    Set-AzureStaticVNetIP -IPAddress "10.20.1.6" |
    Update-AzureVM

Get-AzureVM -ServiceName $serviceName -Name vnetjoinedvm4 |
    Set-AzureStaticVNetIP -IPAddress "10.20.1.7" |
    Update-AzureVM


# Regardless of the start order, the virtual machines will have
# the correct IP addresses
Start-AzureVM -ServiceName $serviceName -Name "vnetjoinedvm4"
Start-AzureVM -ServiceName $serviceName -Name "vnetjoinedvm1"
Start-AzureVM -ServiceName $serviceName -Name "vnetjoinedvm2"
Start-AzureVM -ServiceName $serviceName -Name "vnetjoinedvm3"
```

```
PS C:\Users\Michael> get-azurevm -ServiceName $serviceName | select Name, IpAddress

Name                                            IpAddress
----                                            ---------
vnetjoinedvm1                                   10.20.1.4
vnetjoinedvm2                                   10.20.1.5
vnetjoinedvm3                                   10.20.1.6
vnetjoinedvm4                                   10.20.1.7
```

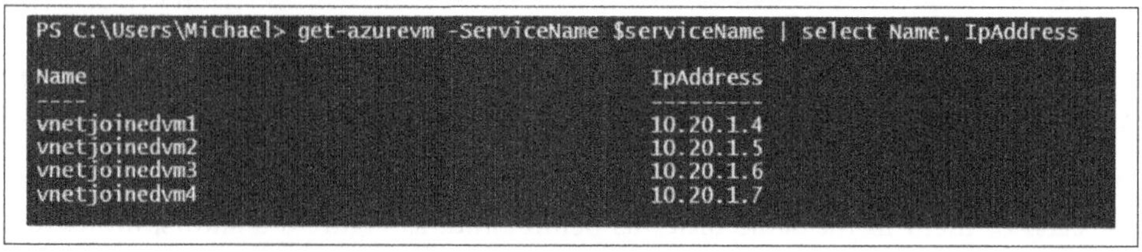

Figure 6-5. Name and IP address assignment with modified start order and static IPs

It is easy to see the static IP address assigned to a virtual machine. Run the Get-AzureVM cmdlet and pipe the output to the Get-AzureStaticVNetIP cmdlet (see Example 6-19 and Figure 6-6).

Example 6-19. Viewing the static IP address of a virtual machine (Console pane)

```
Get-AzureVM -ServiceName $serviceName -Name "vnetjoinedvm1" | Get-AzureStaticVNetIP
```

Figure 6-6. Get-AzureStaticVNetIP output

Removing a static IP address follows the same process as setting one. You must return the virtual machine configuration by using the Get-AzureVM cmdlet, modify it through the PowerShell pipeline by using Remove-AzureStaticVNetIP, and then send the modified configuration back by using the Update-AzureVM cmdlet (see Example 6-20 and Figure 6-7).

Example 6-20. Removing a static IP address (Console pane)

```
Get-AzureVM -ServiceName $serviceName -Name "vnetjoinedvm4" |
    Remove-AzureStaticVNetIP |
    Update-AzureVM
```

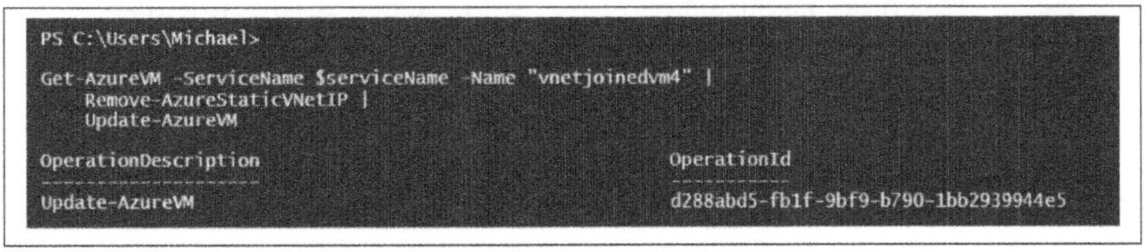

Figure 6-7. Removing a static IP address

Moving Virtual Machines to Different Subnets

Another common network task you will perform with PowerShell is subnet migration. For example, if I wanted to use one of the previously created virtual machines as a domain controller on its own subnet, I could use the code shown in Example 6-21 to move it from the AppSubnet to the DCSubnet (see Figure 6-8).

Example 6-21. Moving a virtual machine between subnets (Console pane)

```
Get-AzureVM -ServiceName $serviceName -Name "vnetjoinedvm4" |
    Set-AzureSubnet -SubnetNames "DCSubnet" |
    Update-AzureVM
```

Reboot warning

Changing the subnet of a virtual machine will cause a reboot!

```
PS C:\Users\Michael> Get-AzureVM -ServiceName $serviceName -Name "vnetjoinedvm4" |
    Set-AzureSubnet -SubnetNames "DCSubnet" |
    Update-AzureVM

OperationDescription                                OperationId
--------------------                                -----------
Update-AzureVM                                      f1043d3c-9667-912d-9df5-3793883acf2a


PS C:\Users\Michael> get-azurevm -ServiceName $serviceName | select Name, IpAddress

Name                                                IpAddress
----                                                ---------
vnetjoinedvm1                                       10.20.1.4
vnetjoinedvm2                                       10.20.1.5
vnetjoinedvm3                                       10.20.1.6
vnetjoinedvm4                                       10.20.2.4
```

Figure 6-8. Changing the subnet of a virtual machine

Static IPs and moving subnets

If a virtual machine already has a static IP address assigned to it from one subnet, it must be removed before it can be moved to another subnet.

Hybrid Network Connectivity

For hybrid network connectivity, there are three options for connecting your Microsoft Azure Virtual Network to non-cloud-based networks such as your on-premises data center or even your laptop at home (or the coffee shop). These hybrid options are site-to-site, point-to-site, and ExpressRoute. Going into depth for each connectivity option is beyond the scope of this book. However, discussing how to automate each option through PowerShell is not.

Gateway Management

Not comprehensive

This section will touch on many virtual network-related topics such as supported devices, gateway types, and virtual network schema. The focus is on using PowerShell to automate these features, not necessarily about the features themselves.

Here are two references that should help with a more thorough understanding:

- Gateways and devices: *http://bit.ly/about_VPN_for_VMs*
- Virtual network schema: *http://bit.ly/VN_config_schema*

Each of the three hybrid connectivity options requires the creation of a gateway. A *gateway* is a software-based device running within your Microsoft Azure subscription that provides connectivity through one of the previously mentioned hybrid options. When you provision a gateway, two worker roles are created under the covers, and they are in active/passive mode for high availability. Unlike virtual networks, gateways do include a separate charge that starts the moment the gateway is provisioned.

Gateways come in two flavors: static and dynamic. Static gateways support the only site-to-site connectivity model, while dynamic gateways can support both site-to-site and point-to-site.

Before creating a gateway using PowerShell, you must create a virtual network that has the gateway described in the network configuration XML. If you are automating this portion of the task, you will have to create the `Gateway` element as part of the `Virtual NetworkSite`, similar to how the virtual network was dynamically added at the beginning of the chapter.

Let's examine a complete virtual network configuration using the network configuration XML. Unlike previous examples, I'm not going to treat this as a sample to walk through but more as a reference for how to build your own.

In Example 6-22, two virtual networks are defined in the network configuration: `PSBookVNETS2S` and `PSBookVNETP2S`.

Example 6-22. Creating virtual networks with site-to-site and point-to-site

```
<?xml version="1.0" encoding="utf-8"?>
<NetworkConfiguration xmlns:xsd="http://www.w3.org/2001/XMLSchema"
xmlns:xsi="http://www.w3.org/2001/XMLSchema-instance"
xmlns="http://schemas.microsoft.com/ServiceHosting/2011/07/NetworkConfiguration">

  <VirtualNetworkConfiguration>
    <Dns>
```

```
      <DnsServers>
        <DnsServer name="AD-DC" IPAddress="192.168.1.60" />
      </DnsServers>
    </Dns>
    <LocalNetworkSites>
      <LocalNetworkSite name="ONPREMVPN">
        <AddressSpace>
          <AddressPrefix>192.168.0.0/16</AddressPrefix>
        </AddressSpace>
        <VPNGatewayAddress>96.226.226.148</VPNGatewayAddress>
      </LocalNetworkSite>
    </LocalNetworkSites>
    <VirtualNetworkSites>
      <VirtualNetworkSite name="PSBookVNETS2S" AffinityGroup="PSBookAG">
        <AddressSpace>
          <AddressPrefix>172.16.0.0/16</AddressPrefix>
        </AddressSpace>
        <Subnets>
          <Subnet name="App">
            <AddressPrefix>172.16.0.0/24</AddressPrefix>
          </Subnet>
          <Subnet name="Data">
            <AddressPrefix>172.16.1.0/24</AddressPrefix>
          </Subnet>
          <Subnet name="DNS">
            <AddressPrefix>172.16.2.0/24</AddressPrefix>
          </Subnet>
          <Subnet name="GatewaySubnet">
            <AddressPrefix>172.16.3.0/29</AddressPrefix>
          </Subnet>
        </Subnets>
        <DnsServersRef>
          <DnsServerRef name="AD-DC" />
        </DnsServersRef>
        <Gateway>
          <ConnectionsToLocalNetwork>
            <LocalNetworkSiteRef name="ONPREMVPN">
              <Connection type="IPsec" />
            </LocalNetworkSiteRef>
          </ConnectionsToLocalNetwork>
        </Gateway>
      </VirtualNetworkSite>
      <VirtualNetworkSite name="PSBookVNETP2S" AffinityGroup="PSBookAG">
        <AddressSpace>
          <AddressPrefix>172.16.0.0/16</AddressPrefix>
        </AddressSpace>
        <Subnets>
          <Subnet name="App">
            <AddressPrefix>172.16.0.0/24</AddressPrefix>
          </Subnet>
          <Subnet name="Data">
            <AddressPrefix>172.16.1.0/24</AddressPrefix>
```

```
      </Subnet>
      <Subnet name="DNS">
        <AddressPrefix>172.16.2.0/24</AddressPrefix>
      </Subnet>
      <Subnet name="GatewaySubnet">
        <AddressPrefix>172.16.3.0/29</AddressPrefix>
      </Subnet>
    </Subnets>
    <Gateway>
      <VPNClientAddressPool>
        <AddressPrefix>10.0.0.0/24</AddressPrefix>
      </VPNClientAddressPool>
      <ConnectionsToLocalNetwork />
    </Gateway>
  </VirtualNetworkSite>
 </VirtualNetworkConfiguration>
</NetworkConfiguration>
```

The first virtual network, PSBookVNETS2S, contains a DnsServersRef element. This element refers to a DNS server that is defined outside of the virtual network itself; this means it could be referenced by multiple virtual networks. The DNS server referenced could point to an on-premises server reachable through a VPN tunnel, or it could point to a server in a virtual network. All virtual machines provisioned into this virtual network will be assigned the IP address of this DNS server at boot time. For availability, you can specify more than one DNS server per virtual network.

In the PSBookVNETS2S virtual network, the Gateway element contains a ConnectionsTo LocalNetwork element that references a separate local network configuration. This configuration describes the IP prefixes for a local network and the IP address for the VPN device to reach it. If you are creating a virtual network that has site-to-site connectivity enabled, at least one local network is required.

In the PSBookVNETP2S virtual network, the gateway element contains a VPNClientAd dressPool element. This is the IP prefix that point-to-site client machines will be allocating IP addresses from when they connect and are authenticated. If you are creating a virtual network that has point-to-site connectivity enabled, this element is required.

Site-to-site and point-to-site can coexist
It is possible to create a virtual network that has both ConnectionsTo LocalNetwork and VPNClientAddressPool elements. The gateway for this type of configuration has to be dynamic, but in this configuration connectivity, in both modes is fully supported.

Now that you have a basic understanding of the gateway configurations, you next need to know how to provision the gateways.

Creating and Automating Gateways

Creating a gateway is straightforward. Use the `New-AzureVNetGateway` cmdlet and specify the gateway type (`StaticRouting` or `DynamicRouting`) and the virtual network name with which you want to associate the gateway (see Example 6-23).

Example 6-23. Creating a gateway

```
New-AzureVNetGateway -VNetName "PSBookVNETS2S" -GatewayType DynamicRouting
```

Before you proceed to configuring the device to accept the VPN connection, you must wait until the gateway has been provisioned. The simplest way to validate that the gateway is provisioned is by retrieving its current state using the `Get-AzureVNetGateway` cmdlet and polling the status until the gateway state is set to `Provisioned` (see Example 6-24). This operation may take 20 to 30 minutes to complete.

Example 6-24. Determining when the gateway is provisioned

```
while($true)
{
    Write-Output "Checking Gateway Status"
    $gatewayStatus = Get-AzureVNetGateway $vnetName
    if($gatewayStatus.State -eq "Provisioning")
    {
        Write-Output "Gateway is still provisioning.. "
        Start-Sleep 30
    }
    elseif($gatewayStatus.State -eq "Provisioned")
    {
        Write-Output "Gateway is provisioned.. "
        break
    }
    else
    {
        Write-Error "Gateway is in an unknown state. Cannot Continue."
        Write-Error "GW State:" $gatewayStatus.State
        return
    }
}
```

If you are configuring a site-to-site connection, you can optionally download the configuration script for your device using a direct call to the Microft Azure API. There currently is no native cmdlet for this call, which is why a direct API call is required.

The API to download the VPN device configuration script requires passing the vendor name, platform, and operating system family as parameters to the URI to identify the correct script. Example 6-25 downloads the configuration script for Microsoft's Routing and Remote Access Service (RRAS).

Example 6-25. Downloading a device script

```
$vnetName = "PSBookVNETS2S"
$vendor = "Microsoft Corporation"
$platform = "RRAS"
$osfamily = "Windows Server 2012"

# Calls and downloads the script
$sURI = "https://management.core.windows.net/$subscriptionID/services/networking/"
$sURI += "$vnetName/gateway/vpndeviceconfigscript?vendor=$vendor&platform=$platform"
$sURI += "&osfamily=$osfamily"

$task = $httpClient.GetStringAsync($sURI)
$task.Wait()

if ($task.IsCompleted)
{
    $vpnScript = $task.Result | Out-String
    $vpnScript | Out-File "$PSScriptRoot\VPNDevice.ps1"
}
else
{
    Write-Error "An Error Occurred Downloading VPN Script" + $task.Exception.Message
}
```

When the script is downloaded, it has to be executed on the remote server. If you were downloading a script for a non-Windows platform, this would likely involve executing the script using SSH. However, since this example is downloading for a Windows server using the Routing and Remote Access Service, the script could be executed using remote PowerShell, as Example 6-26 indicates.

Example 6-26. Executing the device script

```
$RRASServer = "myrrassvr"

Write-Output "Configuring RRAS for Site-to-Site tunnel on Server $RRASServer"
Invoke-Command -ComputerName $RRASServer -FilePath "$PSScriptRoot\VPNDevice.ps1"
```

When the gateway is created, it will automatically attempt to connect to the VPN device specified in the network configuration. You can use the Get-AzureVNetConnection cmdlet to monitor the status (see Example 6-27 and Figure 6-9).

Example 6-27. Detecting gateway connection state

```
Get-AzureVNetConnection -VNetName $vnetName
```

At some point you may need to disconnect or reconnect the gateway. The cmdlet to perform these operations is Set-AzureVNetGateway. The cmdlet accepts a -Disconnect parameter to tell it to disconnect, as well as a -Connect parameter to do the opposite (see Example 6-28 and Example 6-29). This cmdlet also requires the virtual network name and the specific local network site (VPN connection) to disconnect or connect.

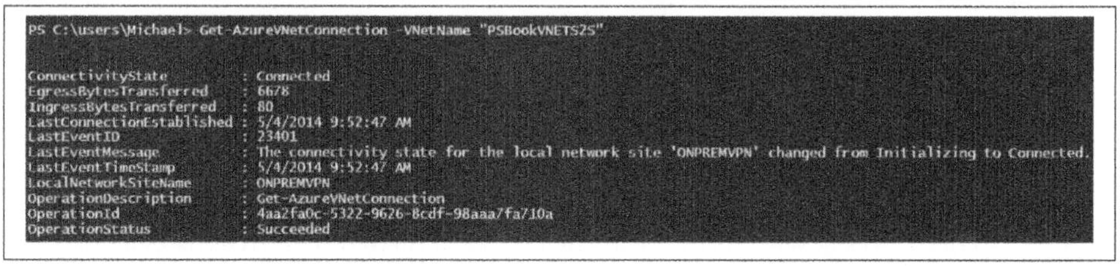

```
PS C:\users\Michael> Get-AzureVNetConnection -VNetName "PSBookVNETS2S"

ConnectivityState         : Connected
EgressBytesTransferred    : 6678
IngressBytesTransferred   : 80
LastConnectionEstablished : 5/4/2014 9:52:47 AM
LastEventID               : 23401
LastEventMessage          : The connectivity state for the local network site 'ONPREMVPN' changed from Initializing to Connected.
LastEventTimeStamp        : 5/4/2014 9:52:47 AM
LocalNetworkSiteName      : ONPREMVPN
OperationDescription      : Get-AzureVNetConnection
OperationId               : 4aa2fa0c-5322-9626-8cdf-98aaa7fa710a
OperationStatus           : Succeeded
```

Figure 6-9. Gateway connection status

Example 6-28. Disconnecting a gateway

```
$siteName = "ONPREMVPN"

Set-AzureVNetGateway -Disconnect -VNetName $vnetName -LocalNetworkSiteName $siteName
```

Example 6-29. Reconnecting a gateway

```
$siteName = "ONPREMVPN"

Set-AzureVNetGateway -Connect -VNetName $vnetName -LocalNetworkSiteName $siteName
```

Gateway charges

As long as the VPN gateway is provisioned, you are being charged (connected or not). The only way to stop being charged for the gateway time is to delete it.

The final gateway cmdlet to mention is, of course, the `Remove-AzureVNetGateway` cmdlet. This cmdlet requires the virtual network name as a parameter and will delete the underlying gateway worker roles upon a successfully completed call (see Example 6-30).

Example 6-30. Deleting a gateway

```
Remove-AzureVNetGateway -VNetName $vnetName
```

Using the Internal Load Balancer

A feature that works hand-in-hand with hybrid connectivity is the internal load balancer. This feature enables two key workloads that are relatively difficult to simulate without a native load balancer.

Intranet workloads

The first workload is the intranet workload. Using the internal load balancer, it is possible to deploy an intranet workload into virtual machines and access those virtual machines from an internal IP address without browsing from the public VIP. These workloads can be accessed over ExpressRoute, site-to-site; or for development, test, and administration over point-to-site (see Figure 6-10).

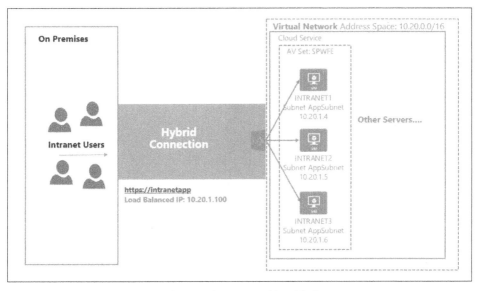

Figure 6-10. Intranet workload using the internal load balancer

N-tier workloads

The second workload that is now enabled is the classic n-tier design pattern, where a middle-tier application server is load-balanced from requests from a frontend web or application tier. This architecture is possible without the internal load balancer by using the external load balancer and access control lists (ACLs), but it fundamentally makes more sense to use the internal IP and not worry about the additional complexities of applying ACLs to your endpoints (see Figure 6-11).

To set up the internal load balancer at virtual machine creation time, you must create an internal load-balancer configuration object that specifies an IP address from a subnet in your virtual network to use as the internal virtual IP address (VIP) and the name of the load balancer.

When specifying the load-balanced endpoints at creation time, the configuration object must be specified when you create the first virtual machine in the deployment as part of the call to New-AzureVM. Virtual machines created in the same cloud service can have load-balanced endpoints that reference the load balancer. These load-balanced endpoints are accessible only from the virtual network itself or from a connected on-premises network.

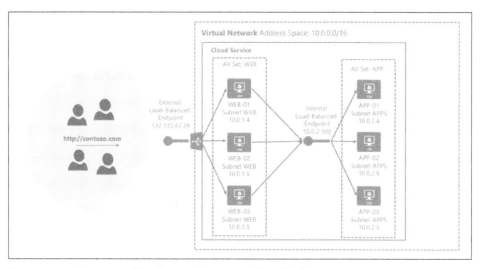

Figure 6-11. N-tier workload using the internal load balancer

Example 6-31 creates a new internal load-balancer configuration object named `MyILB`. This object points to an IP address in the AppSubnet subnet from the previously referenced virtual network.

If you would like to try this experiment out on your own, you should first delete any virtual machines you may have created in the `PSBookVNET` virtual network. Then, using your PowerShell ISE, create a new PowerShell script named *chapter6ilb.ps1* and add the following code.

Example 6-31. Creating an internal load-balancer configuration object (Script pane)

```
$ilb = New-AzureInternalLoadBalancerConfig -InternalLoadBalancerName "MyILB" `
                            -StaticVNetIPAddress "10.20.1.100" `
                            -SubnetName "AppSubnet"
```

The next step after creating the internal load-balancer configuration object is to create a set of virtual machines with load-balanced endpoints. These endpoints will be bound to the IP address specified in the configuration for load balancing. Replace the placeholder values with your own values and ensure that you use a new unique cloud service name (see Example 6-32).

Example 6-32. Creating a set of virtual machines using the internal load balancer (Script pane)

```
# Specify the cloud service
$serviceName = "[cloud service name]"

# Specify the admin credentials
```

```
$adminUser = "[admin username]"
$password = "[admin password]"

# Specify the region (must match the same region as your virtual network)
$location = "[region name]"

# Specify the virtual machine names
$vmName1 = "intranet1"
$vmName2 = "intranet2"

$vmSize = "Small"
$vnetName = "PSBookVNET"
$imageFamily = "Windows Server 2012 R2 Datacenter"

$imageName = Get-AzureVMImage |
                where { $_.ImageFamily -eq $imageFamily } |
                sort PublishedDate -Descending |
                select -ExpandProperty ImageName -First 1

# Create a virtual machine configuration object
$vm1 = New-AzureVMConfig -Name $vmName1 -InstanceSize $vmSize -ImageName $imageName

$vm1 | Add-AzureProvisioningConfig -Windows `
                                  -AdminUsername $adminUser `
                                  -Password $password

$vm1 | Set-AzureSubnet -SubnetNames "AppSubnet"

$vm1 | Add-AzureEndpoint -Name "intranet" -Protocol tcp `
                        -LocalPort 80 -PublicPort 80 `
                        -LBSetName "lbintranet" `
                        -InternalLoadBalancerName "MyILB" `
                        -DefaultProbe

# Create a virtual machine configuration object
$vm2 = New-AzureVMConfig -Name $vmName2 -InstanceSize $vmSize -ImageName $imageName

$vm2 | Add-AzureProvisioningConfig -Windows `
                                  -AdminUsername $adminUser `
                                  -Password $password

$vm2 | Set-AzureSubnet -SubnetNames "AppSubnet"

$vm2 | Add-AzureEndpoint -Name "intranet" -Protocol tcp `
                        -LocalPort 80 -PublicPort 80 `
                        -LBSetName "lbintranet" `
                        -InternalLoadBalancerName "MyILB" `
                        -DefaultProbe

# Specify the internal load balancer configuration and the virtual network
New-AzureVM -ServiceName $serviceName `
            -Location $location `
```

```
-VNetName $vnetName `
-InternalLoadBalancerConfig $ilb `
-VMs $vm1, $vm2
```

Subnets and the internal load balancer
The internal load balancer's static IP address must be on the same subnet as the virtual machines to which you are adding load-balanced endpoints.

Validating the internal load balancer

An easy way to validate that the internal load balancer is indeed working is to log in to each virtual machine and install IIS. Modify the default HTML file in *C:\inetpub\wwwroot\iisstart.htm* to contain the server name (intranet1 or intranet2). Create a third virtual machine in the virtual network by using the portal or PowerShell. From that virtual machine, you can modify the hosts file to contain a mapping to the internal VIP. An example host file entry is `10.20.1.100 myintranet`.

Updating internal load-balanced endpoints

Updating endpoints using the internal load balancer is exactly the same as you learned about in Chapter 4 with regular load-balanced endpoints. The `Set-AzureLoadBalancedEndpoint` cmdlet works against endpoints that are internally load-balanced the same way that it does against external load-balanced endpoints.

There can be only one

There can be only one internal load-balancer configuration with each virtual machine deployment (cloud service). If you need multiple configurations, simply create a new cloud service in the same virtual network with a new configuration.

Adding an internal load balancer to an existing deployment

You can add an internal load balancer to an existing virtual machine deployment (assuming one does not already exist) by using the `Add-AzureInternalLoadBalancer` cmdlet. This cmdlet accepts the same parameters that `New-AzureInternalLoadBalancerConfig` does with the addition of the `-ServiceName` parameter to specify the existing cloud service to which to add the configuration. When the configuration is added, you can use the `Add-AzureEndpoint` cmdlet to add the internal load-balanced endpoints.

Removing an internal load balancer from an existing deployment

You can also remove the internal load balancer from an existing virtual machine deployment by using the `Remove-AzureInternalLoadBalancer` cmdlet. Specify the cloud service by using the `-ServiceName` parameter, and it will be removed. You do need to first remove any endpoints that reference the internal load balancer.

Viewing the internal load-balancer configuration on an existing deployment

Since you can add and remove, it only makes sense that you can view the configuration as well. Use the `Get-AzureInternalLoadBalancer` cmdlet and pass the cloud service name to the `-ServiceName` parameter to view the current configuration.

ExpressRoute

I have saved the best for last (at least from a capabilities perspective). Microsoft Azure ExpressRoute is a hybrid connectivity technology that allows you to have a private, low-latency direct connection from your data center (or colocated data center) directly to Microsoft Azure. The cmdlets to configure ExpressRoute are relatively straightforward.

Before you can execute Azure ExpressRoute cmdlets, you need to load the ExpressRoute module directly by using the `Import-Module` cmdlet (see Example 6-33).

Example 6-33. Loading the ExpressRoute PowerShell module (path split for readability)

```
$m = "C:\Program Files (x86)\Microsoft SDKs\Azure\PowerShell\ServiceManagement\"
$m += "Azure\ExpressRoute\ExpressRoute.psd1"
Import-Module $m
```

The first cmdlet you should know about with ExpressRoute is `Get-AzureDedicatedCircuitServiceProvider`. This cmdlet enumerates the available providers, locations, and bandwidth capabilities (see Example 6-34 and Figure 6-12).

Example 6-34. Identifying ExpressRoute providers

```
Get-AzureDedicatedCircuitServiceProvider
```

At this point, if you do not have a relationship with one of these providers already, you need to reach out to them to set up an agreement. Either you will need your own cage with servers in place at an exchange provider or you will need to work with a network service provider for services through an MPLS VPN.

Assuming that the contracts and technical setup for your partner connection are in place, the next task you need to complete is to create an ExpressRoute circuit. A circuit defines the connectivity parameters between your network and Microsoft Azure.

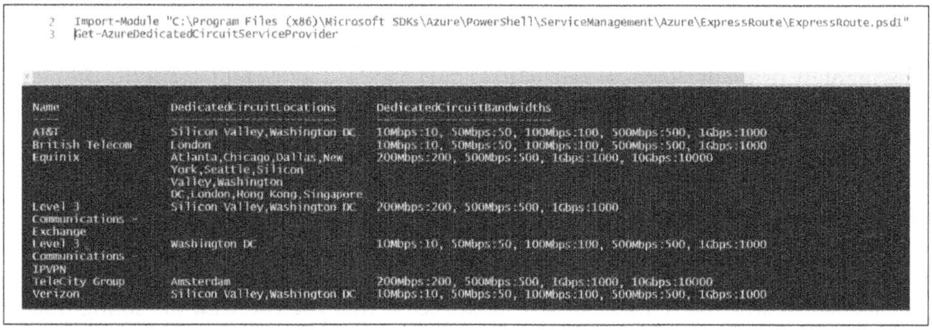

```
  2   Import-Module "C:\Program Files (x86)\Microsoft SDKs\Azure\PowerShell\ServiceManagement\Azure\ExpressRoute\ExpressRoute.psd1"
  3   Get-AzureDedicatedCircuitServiceProvider
```

Name	DedicatedCircuitLocations	DedicatedCircuitBandwidths
AT&T	Silicon Valley,Washington DC	10Mbps:10, 50Mbps:50, 100Mbps:100, 500Mbps:500, 1Gbps:1000
British Telecom	London	10Mbps:10, 50Mbps:50, 100Mbps:100, 500Mbps:500, 1Gbps:1000
Equinix	Atlanta,Chicago,Dallas,New York,Seattle,Silicon Valley,Washington DC,London,Hong Kong,Singapore	200Mbps:200, 500Mbps:500, 1Gbps:1000, 10Gbps:10000
Level 3 Communications - Exchange	Silicon Valley,Washington DC	200Mbps:200, 500Mbps:500, 1Gbps:1000
Level 3 Communications IPVPN	Washington DC	10Mbps:10, 50Mbps:50, 100Mbps:100, 500Mbps:500, 1Gbps:1000
TeleCity Group	Amsterdam	200Mbps:200, 500Mbps:500, 1Gbps:1000, 10Gbps:10000
Verizon	Silicon Valley,Washington DC	10Mbps:10, 50Mbps:50, 100Mbps:100, 500Mbps:500, 1Gbps:1000

Figure 6-12. Enumerating ExpressRoute providers

Once you know the available bandwidth, provider name, and location, you have everything you need to create an ExpressRoute circuit (see Example 6-35 and Figure 6-13).

Example 6-35. Creating an ExpressRoute circuit

```
New-AzureDedicatedCircuit -CircuitName "1GbpsCircuit" `
                          -Bandwidth 1024 `
                          -Location "Silicon Valley" `
                          -ServiceProviderName "Equinix"
```

```
PS C:\> New-AzureDedicatedCircuit -CircuitName "1GbpsCircuit" -Bandwidth 1024 -Location "Silicon Valley" -ServiceProviderName "equinix"

Bandwidth                        : 1024
CircuitName                      : 1GbpsCircuit
Location                         : Silicon Valley
ServiceKey                       : 7d117b16-5bcd-4462-a48a-88a5e430ca08
ServiceProviderName              : equinix
ServiceProviderProvisioningState : NotProvisioned
Status                           : Enabled
```

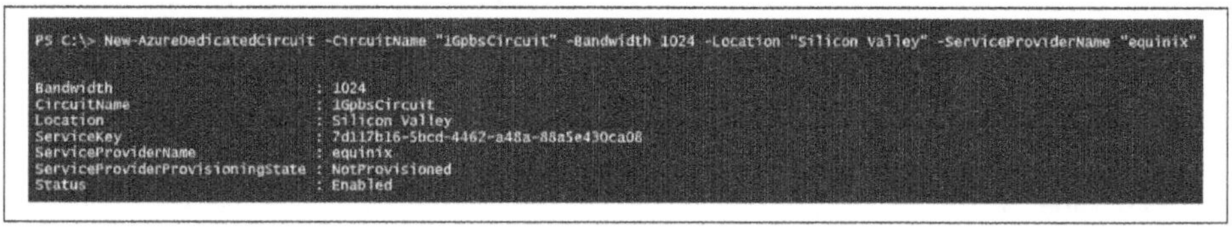

Figure 6-13. Creating a new circuit

Billing starts now!

The moment you execute the `New-AzureDedicatedCircuit` cmdlet successfully, Microsoft Azure will start billing your subscription. Be prepared to engage your provider *immediately* after to avoid being charged for a circuit that is not in use.

When the ExpressRoute circuit has been created, your next step is to contact your service provider. If this provider is a network service provider, they will perform configuration for routing and configure ExpressRoute to be available to your network.

If your provider is an exchange provider, it is up to you to configure routing. This configuration needs to take place with your routers hosted in your cage, and you also need to tell Microsoft Azure how your router is configured. Registering your router configuration with Microsoft Azure is possible through PowerShell.

Configuring BGP routing in full detail is beyond the scope of this book, and I would refer you back to the Microsoft Azure ExpressRoute documentation (*http://bit.ly/ ExpressRoute_docs*) for more details.

The New-AzureBGPPeering cmdlet tells Microsoft Azure what the IP addresses for your routers are by passing them via the -PrimaryPeerSubnet and -SecondaryPeerSubnet parameters. Each subnet represents the IP addresses that one of your routers is configured on and it also tells Microsoft Azure the IP address that you want the routers in Azure to use.

In Example 6-36, the primary subnet 172.16.1.0/30 tells Microsoft Azure that your primary router will be listening on 172.16.1.1 and that you would like the Microsoft Azure router to listen on 172.16.1.2 (the remaining IP addresses on the subnet are reserved).

The secondary subnet is for your secondary router. You should have two physical routers for high availability and to be in compliance for the ExpressRoute service-level agreement (SLA).

The New-AzureBGPPeering cmdlet also can accept the -AccessType parameter, which represents either private or public peering (the default is private). Configuring private peering tells Microsoft Azure to publish any virtual network IP addresses that are later linked to the circuit to your router. This allows traffic between your on-premises network and your virtual network to be routed over your ExpressRoute circuit. Specifying Public for this value tells Microsoft Azure to publish routes for all Microsoft Azure public services to your routers. This has the effect of providing connectivity between your on-premises network and Microsoft Azure public services—such as storage and SQL Database—using your private ExpressRoute circuit instead of going across the public Internet.

You will need several other parameters as well that you should know from when you configured your routers. For instance, you should specify a password to ensure that only your routers can participate in exchanging routes. You must also specify an autonomous system number (ASN) that represents the network for which your routers can exchange routes. Finally, you must specify separate VLAN IDs for private and public peering.

Example 6-36 shows how you could potentially configure BGP routing between your exchange provider network and Microsoft Azure.

Example 6-36. Configuring BGP routing for an exchange provider

```
# Service key from your previously created and provisioned circuit
$ServiceKey = "[your service key goes here]"

# MD5 hash to authenticate BGP sessions
$MD5Hash = "[your MD5 hash password]"
```

```
# Subnets used for configuring private peering
$private_Subnet_Primary   = "172.16.1.0/30"
$private_Subnet_Secondary = "172.16.2.0/30"

# Subnets used for configuring public peering
$public_Subnet_Primary    = "172.16.1.4/30"
$public_Subnet_Secondary  = "172.16.2.4/30"

# Autonomous System Number
$ASN = "65520"

# VLAN ID for private peering
$VLANPrivate = "555"

# VLAN ID for public peering
$VLANPublic = "556"

# Create the private peering configuration
New-AzureBGPPeering -ServiceKey $ServiceKey `
                    -PrimaryPeerSubnet $private_Subnet_Primary `
                    -SecondaryPeerSubnet $private_Subnet_Secondary `
                    -PeerAsn $ASN `
                    -VlanId $VLANPrivate `
                    -AccessType Private `
                    -SharedKey $MD5Hash


# Create the public peering configuration
New-AzureBGPPeering -ServiceKey $ServiceKey `
                    -PrimaryPeerSubnet $public_Subnet_Primary `
                    -SecondaryPeerSubnet $public_Subnet_Secondary `
                    -PeerAsn $ASN `
                    -VlanId $VLANPublic `
                    -AccessType Public `
                    -SharedKey $MD5Hash
```

To view the existing BGP configuration, you can use the `Get-AzureBGPPeering` cmdlet (see Example 6-37 and Figure 6-14). This cmdlet accepts a `-ServiceKey` and, optionally, the `-AccessType` (the default is private).

Example 6-37. Viewing BGP peering configuration for an ExpressRoute circuit

```
# Show private peering configuration
Get-AzureBGPPeering -ServiceKey $serviceKey

# Shows public peering configuration
Get-AzureBGPPeering -ServiceKey $serviceKey -AccessType Public
```

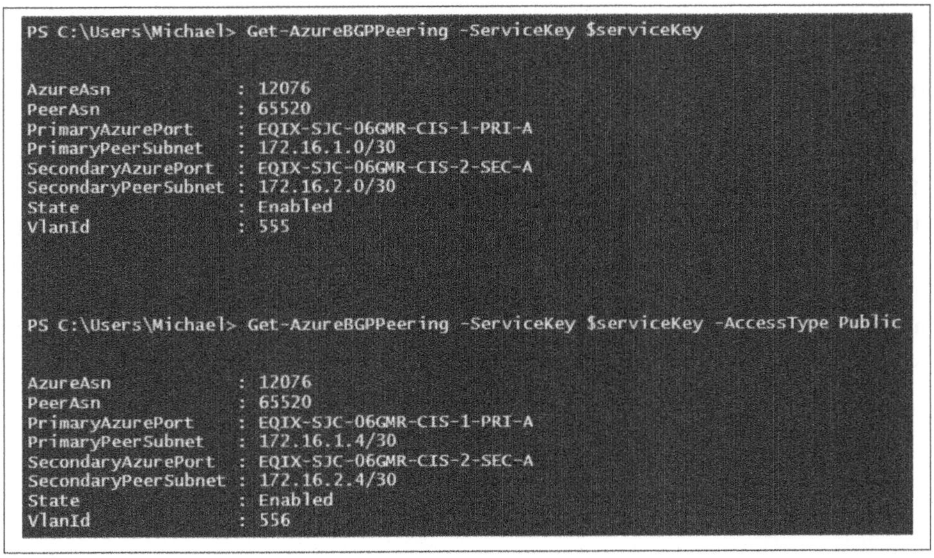

```
PS C:\Users\Michael> Get-AzureBGPPeering -ServiceKey $serviceKey


AzureAsn             : 12076
PeerAsn              : 65520
PrimaryAzurePort     : EQIX-SJC-06GMR-CIS-1-PRI-A
PrimaryPeerSubnet    : 172.16.1.0/30
SecondaryAzurePort   : EQIX-SJC-06GMR-CIS-2-SEC-A
SecondaryPeerSubnet  : 172.16.2.0/30
State                : Enabled
VlanId               : 555



PS C:\Users\Michael> Get-AzureBGPPeering -ServiceKey $serviceKey -AccessType Public


AzureAsn             : 12076
PeerAsn              : 65520
PrimaryAzurePort     : EQIX-SJC-06GMR-CIS-1-PRI-A
PrimaryPeerSubnet    : 172.16.1.4/30
SecondaryAzurePort   : EQIX-SJC-06GMR-CIS-2-SEC-A
SecondaryPeerSubnet  : 172.16.2.4/30
State                : Enabled
VlanId               : 556
```

Figure 6-14. Viewing BGP peering configuration

The final cmdlet to use with Microsoft Azure ExpressRoute is the New-AzureDedicatedCircuitLink cmdlet (see Figure 6-15). This cmdlet accepts the -ServiceKey that uniquely identifies your circuit and a virtual network that you would like to link to the circuit. You can link multiple virtual networks to your ExpressRoute circuits, as long as the virtual network and circuit are on the same continent.

When you link the virtual network, as shown in Example 6-38, Microsoft Azure will then publish the routes to your private address space to your on-premises routers. It is important that you wait until your service provider has completed provisioning before executing this command.

Example 6-38. Linking a virtual network to an ExpressRoute circuit

```
New-AzureDedicatedCircuitLink -ServiceKey $serviceKey -VNetName $vnetName
```

```
PS C:\Users\Michael> New-AzureDedicatedCircuitLink -ServiceKey $serviceKey -VNetName $vnetName

                                                     State VnetName
                                                     ----- --------
                                                 Provisioned ExpressRouteVNET
```

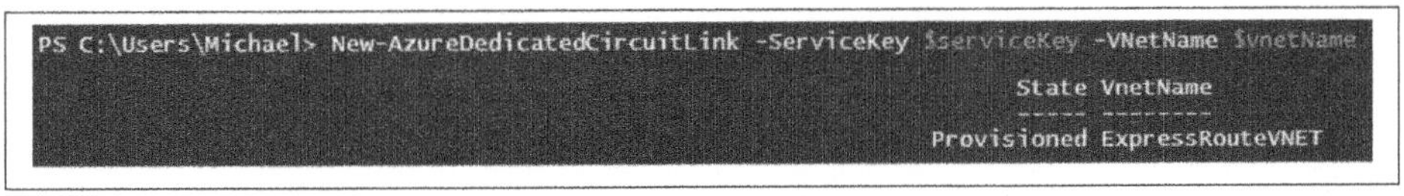

Figure 6-15. Linking a virtual network to the provisioned circuit

Summary

In this chapter we explored Microsoft Azure Virtual Networks from the perspective of a PowerShell user. You learned that to automate the modification of your virtual networking configuration, you need to brush up on your PowerShell XML skills and use the `Get-AzureVNetConfig` and `Set-AzureVNetConfig` cmdlets. From there, we discussed how to provision gateways and view their status. We also covered how to configure internal load balancing, which can be used for intranet or load-balanced middle-tier workloads. Finally, we ended the discussion on the newest member of the networking family, ExpressRoute. In the next chapter we will discuss several advanced techniques for automating virtual machines.

## CHAPTER 7

Advanced Virtual Machines

This final chapter will cover the advanced features of virtual machine provisioning, virtual machine extensions, remote PowerShell, and some tips and tricks I have found that can be very useful when managing virtual machines.

Virtual Machine Provisioning

The provisioning engine for Microsoft Azure Virtual Machines has several features that can be used in certain situations that have not yet been discussed in detail. For instance, you can provision Linux-based virtual machines, you can set the time zone, enable or disable Windows Update, enable or disable remote management options, domain-join a virtual machine, and even specify certificates to be automatically uploaded and deployed on your behalf.

Some of the provisioning settings can be specified with `New-AzureQuickVM` and some only when composing a virtual machine with `New-AzureVMConfig`, `Add-AzureProvisioningConfig`, and `New-AzureVM`. I'll tackle these one at a time using the PowerShell cmdlets and highlight how they can be used.

Provisioning Linux Virtual Machines

One of the first surprises to many new users of Microsoft Azure is the extent of support for Linux-based virtual machines. Microsoft has embraced openness in its cloud-computing platform with support of Linux and various open source languages and developer frameworks. With this in mind, it should not come as a total surprise that the PowerShell cmdlets also have rich support for provisioning virtual machines based on Linux (see Example 7-1 and Figure 7-1).

You can view the images available by using the `Get-AzureVMImage` cmdlet and filtering on the `OS` property to show only the Linux images.

Example 7-1. Viewing available Linux images (Console pane)

```
Get-AzureVMImage | where OS -eq "Linux" | sort PublishedDate -Descending
```

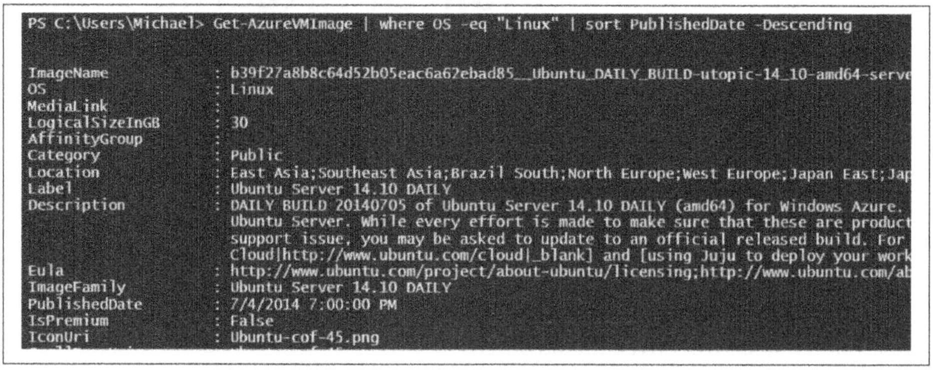

Figure 7-1. Linux images

At a high level, provisioning a Linux-based virtual machine is not significantly different from provisioning a Windows-based virtual machine. There are some differences in the more advanced provisioning options, but at the simplest level they are almost identical.

You can provision a Linux virtual machine by using username and password authentication; specifying an SSH certificate is also supported. To try out creating a Linux-based virtual machine with a username and password, create a new PowerShell script named *chapter7linuxuserpass.ps1* and add the code shown in Example 7-2. Ensure that you change the placeholder values with real values.

Example 7-2. Creating a Linux virtual machine with username and password (Script pane)

```
$subscription = "[subscription name]"
$linuxUser = "[username]"
$password = "[your password]"
$serviceName = "[cloud service name]"
$location = "[region name]"
$vmSize = "Small"

Select-AzureSubscription $subscription

$vmName = "linuxVM1"

$imageFamily = "Ubuntu Server 14.10 DAILY"

$imageName = Get-AzureVMImage |
             where { $_.ImageFamily -eq $imageFamily } |
             sort PublishedDate -Descending |
```

```
                select -ExpandProperty ImageName -First 1
```

```
New-AzureVMConfig -Name $vmName -InstanceSize $vmSize -ImageName $imageName |
    Add-AzureProvisioningConfig -Linux -LinuxUser $linuxUser -Password $password |
    New-azureVM -ServiceName $serviceName -Location $location
```

Execute the script by pressing F5 or by highlighting all of the text and pressing F8. When the virtual machine has completed provisioning, you can connect using SSH with the username and password specified.

Provisioning Linux virtual machines by using an SSH certificate requires you to create the SSH certificate first. The SSH certificate must be encapsulated within an X509 certificate for the provisioning engine. For details on creating the SSH certificate in this fashion, the Microsoft Azure documentation (*http://bit.ly/SSH_to_Linux_VMs*) will be the best place to start.

Deploying the certificate from PowerShell requires a slightly different process than we have seen from previous examples of virtual machine creation. The SSH certificate must be installed on the cloud service container first to be referenced and deployed to the virtual machine. This means that if you are creating the first virtual machine in the cloud service, the creation of the cloud service and the creation of the virtual machine need to be split into separate operations.

In the following example, the cloud service is created first by using the New-AzureService cmdlet, and the SSH certificate is uploaded to the cloud service by using the Add-AzureCertificate cmdlet.

The association of the certificate to the Linux virtual machine as an SSH key is made using the New-AzureSSHKey cmdlet. This cmdlet simply makes a configuration object that maps the certificate to be deployed on the virtual machine when it is provisioned.

To try out creating a Linux-based virtual machine with a username, password, and SSH certificate, create a new PowerShell script named *chapter7linuxsshcert.ps1* and add the code shown in Example 7-3. Ensure that you replace the placeholder values with real values. Since this example creates the cloud service, you should specify a new, unique cloud service name.

Example 7-3. Creating a Linux virtual machine with an SSH certificate (Script pane)

```
$subscription = "[subscription name]"
$linuxUser = "[username]"
$password = "[your password]"
$serviceName = "[cloud service name]"
$location = "[region name]"
$vmSize = "Small"

# Ensure you have created the certificate - example C:\Scripts\mycert.cer
# http://azure.microsoft.com/en-us/documentation/articles/linux-use-ssh-key/
```

```
$certPath = "[path to your certificate]"

Select-AzureSubscription $subscription

New-AzureService -ServiceName $serviceName -Location $location

Add-AzureCertificate -CertToDeploy $certPath -ServiceName $serviceName

$cert = Get-PfxCertificate -FilePath $certPath

# Create a certificate in the user's home directory
$sshkey = New-AzureSSHKey -PublicKey -Fingerprint $cert.Thumbprint `
                          -Path "/home/$linuxUser/.ssh/authorized_keys"


$vmName = "linuxVMSSH"

$imageFamily = "Ubuntu Server 14.10 DAILY"

$imageName = Get-AzureVMImage |
                where { $_.ImageFamily -eq $imageFamily } |
                sort PublishedDate -Descending |
                select -ExpandProperty ImageName -First 1


New-AzureVMConfig -Name $vmName -InstanceSize $vmSize -ImageName $imageName |
    Add-AzureProvisioningConfig -Linux -LinuxUser $linuxUser `
                                -Password $password -SSHPublicKeys $sshkey |
    New-AzureVM -ServiceName $serviceName
```

Using only SSH certificates
In the Linux world it is common practice to not log in with a username and password at all and authenticate using only an SSH certificate. To accomplish this with PowerShell, you can specify the
-NoSSHPassword parameter, and only certificate authentication will
be available.

Availability Sets

An *availability set* is a feature used with Microsoft Azure Virtual Machines that allows
you to group virtual machines that perform identical workloads into a logical grouping
that tells Microsoft Azure to treat them in a highly available manner.

What does it mean to treat two virtual machines in a highly available manner? To answer,
let's take a look at a possible deployment of two web servers (IISVM1 and IISVM2) in
a Microsoft Azure data center without using an availability set (see Figure 7-2).

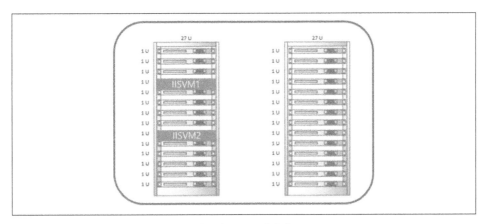

Figure 7-2. Virtual machines outside of an availability set

The two virtual machines could be deployed on the same physical rack in the data center. This means that there are single points of failure, such as the power supply and the top of the rack switch. This also means that Microsoft Azure has no knowledge of which virtual machines are performing the same workload. Microsoft Azure needs to know that your virtual machines are performing the same workload because it periodically updates the host machines that are hosting your virtual machines. When this happens, the host machines require rebooting. This means that your servers will also be rebooted as part of the host update process.

With the knowledge of which servers are performing the same workload, Microsoft Azure can reboot them in an intelligent manner and not take all of them down at the same time to cause your deployment downtime.

In addition to performing intelligent host updates, virtual machines grouped in an availability set will be deployed onto separate racks in the data center. The number of separate physical racks depends on the number of virtual machines in the availability set (see Figure 7-3). This gives your application high availability at the physical level:

- Redundant power supply
- Redundant network paths
- Redundant physical server

Deploying virtual machines in availability sets is critical for uptime and is, in fact, currently required to achieve the 99.95 percent service-level agreement (SLA) within Microsoft Azure.

For more details on availability sets and the underlying details of how they work, visit the Microsoft Azure documentation center (*http://bit.ly/managing_VM_availability*).

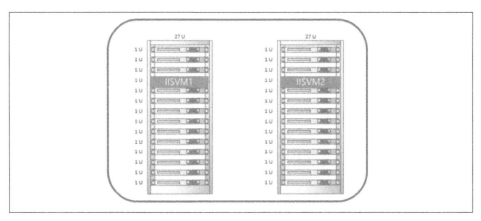

Figure 7-3. Virtual machines deployed in an availability set

Now that you know what an availability set is, how do you put your virtual machines into one?

Provisioning Virtual Machines in an Availability Set

Putting virtual machines into an availability set at creation time is very simple. You just have to specify a name for your availability set by using the `-AvailabilitySetName` parameter, which is supported with `New-AzureVMConfig` and `New-AzureQuickVM`. Each virtual machine that should be part of the same set should be in the same cloud service and created with the same availability set name. All virtual machines performing the same workload that also share the same life cycle should be in the same availability set.

The following example uses a `for` loop to create configuration objects for multiple virtual machines. When the virtual machine configuations are created, the availability set name webavset is assigned to each virtual machine.

To try this on your own, create a new PowerShell script named *chapter7createavset.ps1*. Add the code shown in Example 7-4 to the script and ensure that you replace the placeholder values with real ones.

Example 7-4. Creating multiple virtual machines in an availability set (Script pane)

```
Select-AzureSubscription "[subscription name]"
$adminUser = "[admin username]"
$password = "[admin password]"
$serviceName = "[cloud service name]"
$location = "[region name]"

# The name of the availability set
$avset = "webavset"
$vmSize = "Small"
$imageFamily = "Windows Server 2012 R2 Datacenter"
```

```
$imageName = Get-AzureVMImage |
            where { $_.ImageFamily -eq $imageFamily } |
            sort PublishedDate -Descending |
            select -ExpandProperty ImageName -First 1


$vmConfigs = @()

for($i=1; $i -le 2; $i++)
{
    # Change the VM name to match the instance number
    $vmName = "webserver$i"

    $vmConfig = New-AzureVMConfig -Name $vmName `
                                  -InstanceSize $vmSize `
                                  -ImageName $imageName `
                                  -AvailabilitySetName $avset

    $vmConfig | Add-AzureProvisioningConfig -Windows `
                                            -AdminUsername $adminUser `
                                            -Password $password

    $vmConfig | Add-AzureEndpoint -Name "http" `
                                  -Protocol tcp `
                                  -LocalPort 80 `
                                  -PublicPort 80 `
                                  -LBSetName "LBHTTP" `
                                  -DefaultProbe

    $vmConfigs += $vmConfig
}

New-AzureVM -ServiceName $serviceName `
            -Location $Location `
            -VMs $vmConfigs
```

Adding Existing Virtual Machines to an Availability Set

Adding existing virtual machines to an availability set requires the same steps used previously to update a virtual machine:

1. Use `Get-AzureVM` to retrieve the virtual machine configuration.

2. Modify the configuration with the `Set-AzureAvailabilitySet` name.

3. Pass the modified configuration to the `Update-AzureVM` cmdlet.

If you would like to try this for yourself using the virtual machines created in Chapter 3 (or any cloud service with more than one virtual machine), create a new file named *chapter7updateavset.ps1* and add the code shown in Example 7-5 and Figure 7-4. Ensure that you modify the placeholder values to use real values.

Example 7-5. Adding existing virtual machines to an availability set

```
Select-AzureSubscription "[subscription name]"

$serviceName = "[cloud service name]"

Get-AzureVM -ServiceName $serviceName |
    Set-AzureAvailabilitySet -AvailabilitySetName "webavset" |
    Update-AzureVM
```

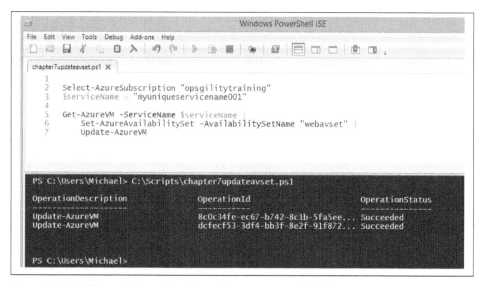

Figure 7-4. Adding existing virtual machines to an availability set

 May cause reboot!
Adding existing virtual machines to an availability set might cause downtime as the Microsoft Azure fabric controller tries to locate appropriate resources and restarts your virtual machine(s).

Specifying the Time Zone

You can set the time zone for a Windows-based virtual machine by using Add-AzureProvisioningConfig, since the provisioning engine under the covers is actually passing parameters using a standard Windows unattended installation. The documentation for unattended install (*http://bit.ly/_TimeZone*) is the best place to look for the correct values.

For example, to create a virtual machine that will be deployed with the Tokyo time zone set, simply specify `-TimeZone "Tokyo Standard Time"` as a parameter to `Add-AzureProvisioningConfig`.

Configuring Windows Update

On Windows-based virtual machines, Windows Update is enabled by default. You can disable it during provisioning time for virtual machines created using an image by specifying the `-DisableAutomaticUpdates` parameter in the call to `Add-AzureProvisioningConfig`.

Deploying Certificates

Image-based deployment with `Add-AzureProvisioningConfig` and `New-AzureQuickVM` both support automatic deployment of certificates. For example, if you need to automatically deploy a certificate for a virtual machine that is available on boot, you can specify a certificate to be automatically uploaded for you.

To deploy a certificate, you need to load the certfcate into an `X509Certifi cate2` .NET object and then pass it to the `-X509Certificates` parameter in the `Add-AzureProvisioningConfig` or the `New-AzureQuickVM` cmdlet. The cmdlets will take the certificate; repackage it as a *.pfx* file in memory, automatically generating the password; and then deploy the certificate to the *Local Machine\MY* certificate store.

Example 7-6 is a partial example of how a certificate could be uploaded and deployed automatically for your virtual machine.

Example 7-6. Certificate deployment example

```
# Assumes the .pfx file is in the same path as the script
$pfxName = Join-Path $PSScriptRoot "MyServerCertificate.pfx"

$cert = New-Object System.Security.Cryptography.X509Certificates.X509Certificate2

$cert.Import($pfxName,$pwd,'Exportable')

$vmConfig | Add-AzureProvisioningConfig -Windows -AdminUserName $user `
                    -Password $adminPwd -X509Certificates $cert
```

Deploying multiple certificates
The `-X509Certificates` parameter accepts an array, so more than one certificate can be specified.

Private keys are exported

By default, deploying a certificate using this method will include the exported private key. To deploy the certificate without the private key, specify the -NoExportPrivateKey parameter.

Managing Access Control Options

Tables 7-1 and 7-2 list several options that you can use for fine-grained control of access to your image-based virtual machines at provisioning time.

Table 7-1. Windows access control options

-ResetPasswordOnFirstLogon	Prompt the administrative user to reset the password on first login.
-NoWinRMEndpoint	Do not create a WinRM (PowerShell remoting) endpoint at all.
-EnableWinRMHttp	Enable WinRM HTTP (off by default). This is for VM-to-VM Remote PowerShell using internal IPs.
-DisableWinRMHttps	Disable PowerShell remoting (HTTPs) (on by default).
-WinRMCertificate	Specify an X509 certificate to use for PowerShell remoting authentication instead of the generated certificate.
-NoRDPEndpoint	Do not create an endpoint for remote desktop.

Table 7-2. Linux access control options

-NoSSHEndpoint	Do not create an endpoint for SSH.
-DisableSSH	Do not enable SSH at all.

The New-AzureQuickVM cmdlet supports a subset of these options related to PowerShell remoting: -NoWinRMEndpoint, -EnableWinRMHttp, -DisableWinRMHttps, and -WinRMCertificate. All of the options can be accessed using the composition model with the Add-AzureProvisioningConfig and New-AzureVM cmdlets.

Domain Join

Using the Microsoft Azure PowerShell cmdlets, you can automatically domain-join a Windows-based virtual machine at provision time. Domain join works by passing domain-join information directly to the unattended install parameters for Windows setup at provision time.

To specify the domain-join information, use the Add-AzureProvisioningConfig cmdlet with the -WindowsDomain parameter. Several properties are required to successfully join a virtual machine to the domain. You will need domain credentials that have rights in Active Directory to join the new computer to the domain, the domain name itself (NetBIOS and fully qualified), and optionally, you may specify an organizational unit (OU) in which to create the new computer account.

Active directory prerequisite
I am not going into detail on how to deploy Active Directory in Microsoft Azure. There is a great tutorial on the Microsoft Azure website (*http://bit.ly/install_Active_Directory*) that covers this in full detail.

Example 7-7 is a partial example that shows how you could use the -WindowsDomain parameter to specify domain-join information for an existing Active Directory deployment. Assuming that the virtual network is configured to reference an Active Directory DNS server when the virtual machine is provisioned, it will automatically join the domain.

Example 7-7. Using the -WindowsDomain parameter for domain join

```
# Domain join information
$domain = "contoso"
$domFQDN = "contoso.com"
$domUser = "[domain admin user]"
$domPass = "[domain password]"
# Adding the virtual machine to an organizational unit is optional
# The OU must already exist
$domOU = 'OU=AzureVMs,DC=contoso,DC=com'
# End domain join information

$serviceName = "[cloud service name]"
$vmName = "[vm name]"
$VNET = "[virtual network name]"
$Subnet = "[subnet name]"
$Location = "[region name]"

$imageFamily = "Windows Server 2012 R2 Datacenter"
$imageName = Get-AzureVMImage |
             where { $_.ImageFamily -eq $imageFamily } |
             sort PublishedDate -Descending |
             select -ExpandProperty ImageName -First 1

$vmConfig = New-AzureVMConfig -Name $vmName -InstanceSize Small `
                              -ImageName $imageName

$vmConfig | Add-AzureProvisioningConfig -WindowsDomain `
                              -AdminUsername $adminUser `
                              -Password $password `
                              -Domain $domain `
                              -JoinDomain $domFQDN `
                              -DomainUserName $domUser `
                              -DomainPassword $domPass `
```

```
                              -MachineObjectOU $domOU

$vmConfig | Set-AzureSubnet -SubnetNames $Subnet

$vmConfig | New-AzureVM -ServiceName $serviceName `
                        -Location $location -VNetName $VNET
```

Using PowerShell Remoting

PowerShell commands can be executed remotely on Windows-based virtual machines. Access can be enabled for connectivity over the Internet by using HTTPS, or virtual machine to virtual machine by using HTTP and internal IP addresses. External access (HTTPS) is enabled by default, and internal access is limited to the default configuration of Windows (which is limited to virtual machines on the same subnet) unless otherwise specified. For external (HTTPS) access, Microsoft Azure will automatically generate a self-signed certificate that you can use to secure your connection to the virtual machine over the Internet. You can specify your own certificate at provisioning time with the -WinRMCertificate if you want to use your own.

You can change the default behavior by specifying the -EnableWinRMHttp parameter at provisioning time to extend the internal WinRM configuration to allow remote commands to work across subnets. You can also pass the -NoWinRMEndpoint or -DisableWinRMHttps parameters to change the default external capabilities for PowerShell.

Enabling PowerShell remoting is a provision-time feature
Specifying -DisableWinRMHttps will tell the provisioning engine to not create the self-signed (or your own) certificate and to not configure WinRM on the virtual machine as part of the provisioning process. There is currently no cmdlet to enable this functionality after the virtual machine has been provisioned.

Configuring a Secure Connection

The first step to secure a PowerShell session is either to deploy your own certificate or to allow Microsoft Azure to generate a self-signed certificate for you.

Deploying your own certificate is as easy as passing an X509Certificate to the -WinRMCertificate parameter of Add-AzureProvisioningConfig or New-AzureQuickVM. If you want to use the automatically generated certificate, there are a few prerequisites.

To use the self-signed certificate generated by Microsoft Azure securely, you need to download that certificate and install it into your local certificate store. The code to do

---

this is fairly complex, so a helper script has been created that can be downloaded from the TechNet Script Center (*http://bit.ly/secure_remote_PowerShell_access*).

Elevation required

The TechNet script requires PowerShell to run elevated because it installs the self-signed certificate into the certificate store of your local machine.

To try this on your own, download the script from the TechNet Script Center gallery into a local directory (I used *C:\Scripts*). When it is downloaded, use the Unblock-File cmdlet to unblock it (Unblock-File "C:\Scripts\InstallWinRMCertAzur eVM.ps1"). Next, create a new elevated PowerShell session. You can launch PowerShell ISE or just *PowerShell.exe* for this example. Finally, to simplify paths from within PowerShell, change the directory to the download folder: CD C:\Scripts.

You will need to specify an existing virtual machine and cloud service that have been deployed using an image (see Example 7-8 and Figure 7-5). I am using one of the virtual machines that was created as part of Chapter 3.

Example 7-8. Using the sample script to enable secure access (Console pane)

```
$subscription = "[subscription name]"
$serviceName  = "[cloud service name]"
$vmName = "ps-vm1"

.\InstallWinRMCertAzureVM.ps1 -SubscriptionName $subscription `
                -ServiceName $serviceName -Name $vmName
```

```
PS C:\Scripts> $subscription = "opsgilitytraining"
PS C:\Scripts> $serviceName = "myuniqueservicename001"
PS C:\Scripts> $vmName = "ps-vm1"
PS C:\Scripts> .\InstallWinRMCertAzureVM.ps1 -SubscriptionName $subscription -ServiceName $serviceName -Name $vmName
Installing WinRM Certificate for remote access: myuniqueservicename001 ps-vm1
PS C:\Scripts>
```

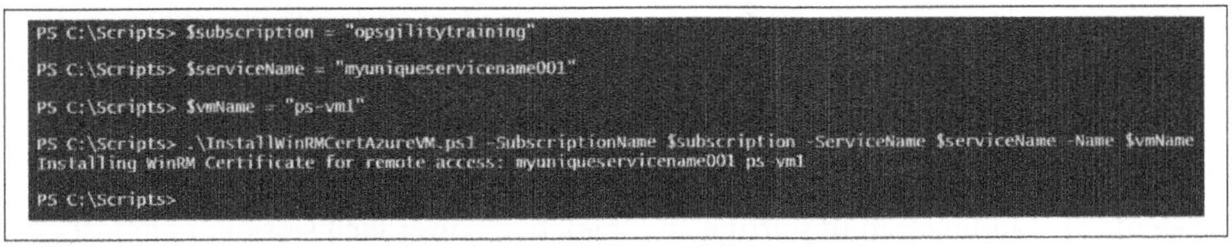

Figure 7-5. Installing the Microsoft Azure-generated certificate

When the script has completed, the certificate is downloaded and installed to your client machine's certificate store. You can now securely connect to the virtual machine in Microsoft Azure by using PowerShell.

You will need to specify the connection URI and credentials to connect to the virtual machine. Get-AzureWinRMUri is a helper cmdlet that queries all of the network endpoints for the specified virtual machine and returns the URI with the public port for the WinRM endpoint. The URI can then be passed to the remote PowerShell cmdlets to open or create a new session or to invoke a script block.

Example 7-9 uses the `Get-AzureWinRMUri` cmdlet to return the remote PowerShell URI and store it in the `$uri` variable. `Get-Credential` is then called to prompt for login credentials for the virtual machine, which are then stored in the `$cred` variable. Both the `$uri` and `$cred` variables are then passed to the `Enter-PSSession` cmdlet, which establishes the remote PowerShell session (see Figure 7-6).

Example 7-9. Entering a remote PowerShell session (Console pane)

```
$uri = Get-AzureWinRMUri -ServiceName $serviceName -Name $vmName

$cred = Get-Credential

Enter-PSSession -ConnectionUri $uri -Credential $cred
```

```
PS C:\Scripts> $uri = Get-AzureWinRMUri -ServiceName $serviceName -Name $vmName

PS C:\Scripts> $cred = Get-Credential
cmdlet Get-Credential at command pipeline position 1
Supply values for the following parameters:

PS C:\Scripts> Enter-PSSession -ConnectionUri $uri -Credential $cred

[myuniqueservicename001.cloudapp.net]: PS C:\Users\demouser\Documents>
```

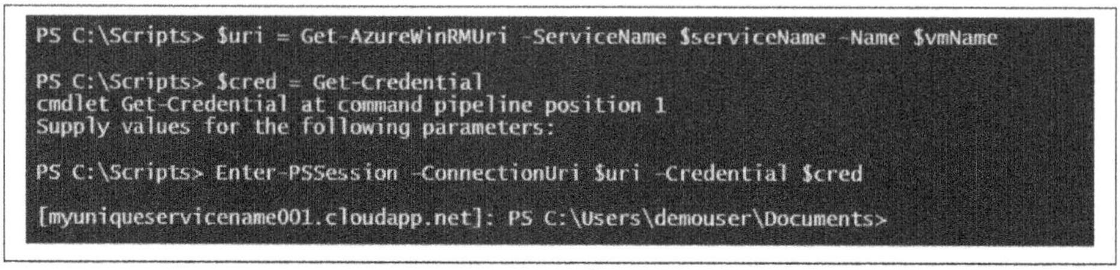

Figure 7-6. Entering a remote PowerShell session

Invoking PowerShell Commands

Using these same techniques, it is easy to execute a PowerShell script remotely on one or more of your virtual machines. Executing commands this way allows you to automate the configuration of roles and features; monitor, download, and install software; update registry settings; or whatever task you can dream up and deliver through PowerShell.

In Example 7-10 I am using the same cmdlets as before—`Get-AzureWinRMUri` and `Get-Credential`—and instead of starting an interactive PowerShell session, I am just executing a script that installs IIS by using the `Invoke-Command` cmdlet (see Figure 7-7). Combine this code with `Get-AzureVM` and you can see how you could easily execute scripts against multiple virtual machines as part of an automation task.

Example 7-10. Executing a script block (Console pane)

```
$uri = Get-AzureWinRMUri -ServiceName $serviceName -Name $vmName

$cred = Get-Credential

Invoke-Command -ConnectionUri $uri `
```

```
-Credential $cred `
-ScriptBlock { Install-WindowsFeature -Name "Web-Server" }
```

```
PS C:\Users\Michael> $uri = Get-AzureWinRMUri -ServiceName $serviceName -Name $vmName

PS C:\Users\Michael> $cred = Get-Credential
cmdlet Get-Credential at command pipeline position 1
Supply values for the following parameters:

PS C:\Users\Michael> Invoke-Command -ConnectionUri $uri -Credential $cred -ScriptBlock { Install-WindowsFeature -Name "Web-Server" }

PSComputerName  : myuniqueservicename001.cloudapp.net
RunspaceId      : 7719ac1c-164a-49d5-889c-145c8ee9a1c5
Success         : True
RestartNeeded   : No
FeatureResult   : {Common HTTP Features, Default Document, Directory Browsing, Request Filtering...}
ExitCode        : Success
```

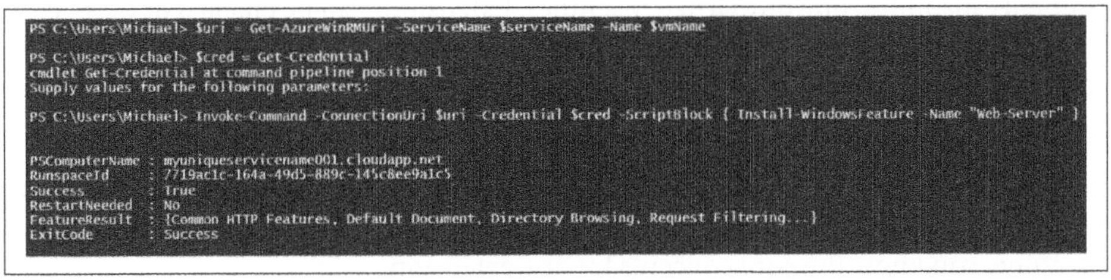

Figure 7-7. Executing a script block to install IIS

The `Invoke-Command` cmdlet can also accept a `-FilePath` parameter, which allows you to specify a file path to a local script instead of a script block. You can also pass parameters using either method with the `-ArgumentList` parameter.

Multiple Hops Using Remote PowerShell

One common problem most people run into when using PowerShell remotely is the multihop dilemma. A remote PowerShell session allows you to execute commands on the computer to which you are connected. This privilege is not delegated to other computers on the remote network by default. This means that for you to access files from a remote file server or to connect to another service using the credentials you used with your PowerShell session, you will be out of luck without additional configuration steps.

If you do need the ability to make multiple hops from your PowerShell session, you can enable CredSSP on your client machine and on the server running your PowerShell session. For more details on how to enable this and the security ramifications involved, see the following articles: *http://bit.ly/multi-hop_support* and *http://bit.ly/CredSSP*.

Virtual Machine Agent and Extensions

By default, Windows-based virtual machines will have the Microsoft Azure Virtual Machine Agent installed when they are provisioned. This agent is a lightweight process that allows for extensibility points or extensions. If you wish to deploy a virtual machine without the agent installed, you just need to pass the `-DisableGuestAgent` parameter to `New-AzureQuickVM` or `Add-AzureProvisioningConfig` at virtual machine creation time. Keep in mind that this is the only way to automatically install the agent. If you want to install the agent outside of the provisioning process, it is a manual option (*http://bit.ly/VM_agent*).

Virtual Machine Extensions

Extensions are written by Microsoft and various third-party publishers to enable additional capabilities on your virtual machines. Extensions can be enabled or disabled at any time by using the correct Get/Set/Remove cmdlet for each extension (assuming you have not provisioned without the virtual machine agent).

In this section, I will review some of the extensions published directly from Microsoft and show how they can be used. Virtual machine extensions follow a similar pattern for deployment. This means that when you learn how to add an extension to a virtual machine, you know the core concepts for any extension.

To see the extensions that are configurable through PowerShell, you can use `Get-Command` to filter on the `Name` property for AzureVM and Extension. The extension cmdlets have a naming convention, where all virtual machine extension cmdlets have AzureVM and Extension built into the name. This makes it easy to identify extension capabilities (see Example 7-11 and Figure 7-8).

Example 7-11. Viewing available virtual machine extensions (Console pane)

```
Get-Command | where { $_.Name -Like "*AzureVM*Extension" }
```

```
PS C:\Users\Michael> Get-Command | where { $_.Name -Like "*AzureVM*Extension" }

CommandType     Name                                          ModuleName
-----------     ----                                          ----------
Cmdlet          Get-AzureVMAccessExtension                     Azure
Cmdlet          Get-AzureVMAvailableExtension                  Azure
Cmdlet          Get-AzureVMBGInfoExtension                     Azure
Cmdlet          Get-AzureVMCustomScriptExtension               Azure
Cmdlet          Get-AzureVMExtension                           Azure
Cmdlet          Get-AzureVMMicrosoftAntimalwareExtension       Azure
Cmdlet          Get-AzureVMPuppetExtension                     Azure
Cmdlet          Remove-AzureVMAccessExtension                  Azure
Cmdlet          Remove-AzureVMBGInfoExtension                  Azure
Cmdlet          Remove-AzureVMCustomScriptExtension            Azure
Cmdlet          Remove-AzureVMExtension                        Azure
Cmdlet          Remove-AzureVMMicrosoftAntimalwareExtension    Azure
Cmdlet          Remove-AzureVMPuppetExtension                  Azure
Cmdlet          Set-AzureVMAccessExtension                     Azure
Cmdlet          Set-AzureVMBGInfoExtension                     Azure
Cmdlet          Set-AzureVMCustomScriptExtension               Azure
Cmdlet          Set-AzureVMExtension                           Azure
Cmdlet          Set-AzureVMMicrosoftAntimalwareExtension       Azure
Cmdlet          Set-AzureVMPuppetExtension                     Azure
```

Figure 7-8. Available virtual machine extensions

Service extensions
You will likely notice another set of extension cmdlets that have AzureService as part of the name instead of AzureVM. These cmdlets are similar to virtual machine extensions except they are designed for Microsoft Azure Cloud Services (web and worker roles).

BgInfo Extension

The `BgInfo` extension is enabled by default when you create a Windows-based virtual machine. The extension simply installs and enables the `Sysinternals BgInfo` utility on the virtual machine to display configuration information for the virtual machine on the desktop (see Figure 7-9).

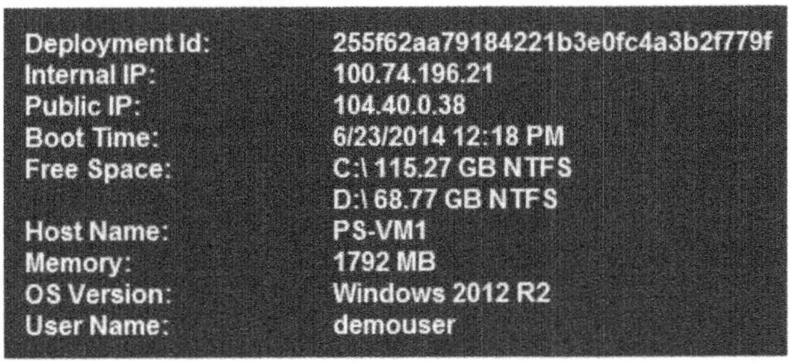

Deployment Id:	255f62aa79184221b3e0fc4a3b2f779f
Internal IP:	100.74.196.21
Public IP:	104.40.0.38
Boot Time:	6/23/2014 12:18 PM
Free Space:	C:\ 115.27 GB NTFS
	D:\ 68.77 GB NTFS
Host Name:	PS-VM1
Memory:	1792 MB
OS Version:	Windows 2012 R2
User Name:	demouser

Figure 7-9. BgInfo

Access Extension

The virtual machine access extension can enable the remote desktop and its associated firewall rule on a virtual machine if it is accidentally (or intentionally) disabled. This extension can also reset the local administrator username and password if they are forgotten.

This extension works in two modes. The first mode is enabling the remote desktop and the associated firewall rules. To execute the extension in this mode, pass the virtual machine configuration to the `Set-AzureVMAccessExtension` cmdlet to enable the extension on the configuration. Then pipe the modified configuration to `Update-AzureVM`. This will trigger a call to execute the extension and allow you back into your virtual machine using the remote desktop (see Example 7-12).

Example 7-12. Enabling remote desktop and firewall rules (Console pane)

```
$serviceName  = "[cloud service name]"
$vmName = "[VM name]"

$vmConfig = Get-AzureVM -ServiceName $serviceName -Name $vmName
```

```
$vmConfig | Set-AzureVMAccessExtension

$vmConfig | Update-AzureVM
```

The second mode allows you to reset the username and password for the local adminstrator account. This is a great feature if you have forgotten either the local admin username or the password, because it allows you to quickly gain access to your virtual machine (see Example 7-13). This extension works only with local accounts. There is no support for resetting domain credentials.

Example 7-13. Resetting the username and password of the local administrator account (Console pane)

```
$serviceName  = "[cloud service name]"
$vmName = "[VM name]"
$newAdminUser = "[new user]"
$newPassword = "[new password]"

$vmConfig = Get-AzureVM -ServiceName $serviceName -Name $vmName

$vmConfig | Set-AzureVMAccessExtension -UserName $newAdminUser -Password $newPassword

$vmConfig | Update-AzureVM
```

Requires a restart

In my testing of the VM access extension, the first time I used the extension to reset the username and password of the local administrator account, the change was immediate. However, in subsequent updates I needed to restart the virtual machine using Restart-AzureVM for the new username and password to be applied.

Custom Script Extension

The virtual machine custom script extension provides the ability to specify a script located in a Microsoft Azure storage account that will be executed on the virtual machine where the extension is executed. You can specify the script to execute at provision time to automatically bootstrap the virtual machine or after provision time as part of an update.

The extension supports passing a string parameter to the script so the customization can be as dynamic as you want to make it.

The best way to learn how this extension works is through a practical example. One of the most common tasks to automate with a virtual machine is to format data disks at boot time. Without automation, this quickly becomes a very tedious task.

Create a new PowerShell script named *ch7formatdisks.ps1* and add the code shown in Example 7-14.

Example 7-14. PowerShell script to format raw disks (Script pane)

```
param(
    $labels
)

# Split the passed-in labels using ; as the delimeter
$labelsArr = $labels.Split(";")

# Format disks
$disks = Get-Disk | where partitionstyle -eq 'raw' | sort number

# Start at F cast to a char
$letters = 70..89 | foreach { ([char] $_ ) }



$count = 0
foreach ($d in $disks) {
  $driveLetter = $letters[$count].ToString()

  $d |
  Initialize-Disk -PartitionStyle MBR -PassThru |
  New-Partition -UseMaximumSize -DriveLetter $driveLetter |
  Format-Volume -FileSystem NTFS -NewFileSystemLabel $labelsArr[$count] `
                -Confirm:$false -Force
  $count++
}
```

As you can see, this code does not contain any references to the Microsoft Azure PowerShell cmdlets. It is a simple PowerShell script that uses the Windows Server storage cmdlets to identify all of the raw disks on the computer and format them. This script does accept a parameter that we can pass in from the extension. To keep things simple, this is a semicolon-delimited string that contains a list of labels to set on the disks as they are formatted.

When you have saved this script locally, you will next need to upload it to Microsoft Azure storage.

Since this book is focused on PowerShell, the following code below will upload the newly created file to a storage account. However, if you feel the need to use a third-party tool with a GUI to upload the file, be my guest.

If you decide to upload the file by using PowerShell, ensure that you specify a valid storage account name (you can use `Get-AzureStorageAccount` to identify your storage accounts) and specify the full path where the folder where you saved the *ch7formatdisks.ps1* script in the `$fileLocation` variable.

The code in Example 7-15 and Figure 7-10 has some lines that are split using the line continuation character (`` ` ``). When executing the commands, they do not have to be split.

Example 7-15. Uploading a script to storage (Console pane)

```
$fileName = "ch7formatdisks.ps1"
$fileLocation = "[full directory path to file (c:\Scripts)]"
$storageAccountName = "[storage account name]"

$filePath = Join-Path $fileLocation $fileName

$Container = "bootstrap"

$storageAccountKey = (Get-AzureStorageKey $storageAccountName).Primary

$context = New-AzureStorageContext -StorageAccountName $StorageAccountName `
                        -StorageAccountKey $storageAccountKey

New-AzureStorageContainer $Container -Permission Container -Context $context

Set-AzureStorageBlobContent -Blob $fileName -Container $Container `
                        -File $filePath -Context $context
```

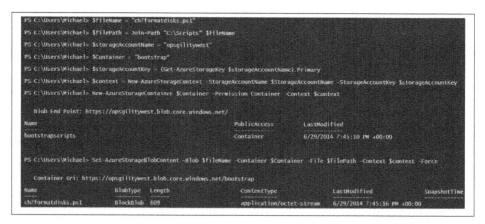

Figure 7-10. Uploading a script to storage

When the script has finished uploading, you can use the `Set-AzureVMCustomScriptExtension` cmdlet on an existing virtual machine or a new virtual machine. This scenario is about formatting disks—a task normally reserved for initial provisioning.

Create a new script using the PowerShell ISE named *ch7bootstrapvm.ps1* and add the code shown in Example 7-16. As always, ensure you replace the placeholder values with real values. The `$storageAccount` variable should contain the name of the storage account where you uploaded the *ch7formatdisks.ps1* script.

Example 7-16. Executing a script at provision time (Script pane)

```
$subscription = "[subscription name]"
$serviceName = "[cloud service name]"
$storageAccount = "[storage account name]"
$location = "[region name]"

Select-AzureSubscription $subscription

# Script file URI
$uri  = "http://$storageAccount.blob.core.windows.net/bootstrap/ch7formatdisks.ps1"
$scriptname = "ch7formatdisks.ps1"

# The number of labels should match the number of data disks you are attaching
$diskLabels = "Label1;Label2"

$size = "Small"
$imageFamily = "Windows Server 2012 R2 Datacenter"
$vmName = "bootstrappedvm"

$imageName = Get-AzureVMImage |
             where { $_.ImageFamily -eq $imageFamily } |
             sort PublishedDate -Descending |
             select -ExpandProperty ImageName -First 1

$cfg = New-AzureVMConfig -Name $vmName -InstanceSize $size -ImageName $imageName

$cfg | Add-AzureProvisioningConfig -Windows `
                       -AdminUsername $adminUser `
                       -Password $password

$cfg | Add-AzureDataDisk -CreateNew -DiskSizeInGB 100 -DiskLabel "Label1" -LUN 0

$cfg | Add-AzureDataDisk -CreateNew -DiskSizeInGB 100 -DiskLabel "Label2" -LUN 1

$cfg | Set-AzureVMCustomScriptExtension -FileUri $uri `
                             -Run $scriptname `
                             -Argument $diskLabels

$cfg | New-AzureVM -ServiceName $serviceName -Location $location
```

Execute the script by pressing F5, or by highlighting the script and pressing F8. When the virtual machine has completed provisioning, log in using remote desktop to validate that the two disks are attached and formatted using the correct drive labels (see Example 7-17 and Figure 7-11).

Example 7-17. Logging in to validate script execution (Console pane)

```
Get-AzureRemoteDesktopFile -ServiceName $serviceName -Name $vmName -Launch
```

Figure 7-11. Automatically formatted data disks at boot

Deleting Virtual Machines

One of the most important concepts to grasp with Microsoft Azure and the cloud in general is the idea that resources are programmable. To be programmable, a resource needs to support some or all of the CRUD properties (create, read, update, and delete) in a programmatic fashion. So far in this book we have seen how to programmatically create, view the configuration, and update a virtual machine by modifying the network, storage, or started state. The final operation to understand is how to delete one or more virtual machines and their associated disk resources.

Deleting a Single Virtual Machine

The simplest method of deleting a virtual machine is to use the `Remove-AzureVM` cmdlet. Similar to `Stop-AzureVM` and `Start-AzureVM`, this cmdlet works directly on the virtual machine and requires you to specify the cloud service name and the virtual machine name to accomplish its task (see Example 7-18).

Example 7-18. Deleting a virtual machine

```
$serviceName = "[cloud service name]"
$vmName = "[VM name]"

Remove-AzureVM -ServiceName $serviceName -Name $vmName
```

When the code is executed, the `Remove-AzureVM` cmdlet will delete the virtual machine and, by default, will leave the OS disk and any data disks alone and untouched. This behavior gives you the option of re-creating the virtual machine at a later date using the same disks.

If you would like the disks to be automatically deleted as part of the virtual machine delete operation, you can also specify the `-DeleteVHD` parameter to `Remove-AzureVM`. The `-DeleteVHD` parameter tells the cmdlet to delete the disks and the underlying VHDs from your storage account. One thing to remember about this parameter is that the delete action is asynchronous. This means that when the virtual machine is deleted, the disks will be automatically deleted some time later by Microsoft Azure (usually within several minutes).

Deleting Multiple Virtual Machines

The previous example showed how to delete a single virtual machine and its associated disks. What if you have an entire environment to delete? PowerShell is known for its amazing ability to automate repetitive tasks such as deleting multiple virtual machines, so let's see how it can be done.

There are two techniques for deleting more than one virtual machine. The first technique is using the `Get-AzureVM` cmdlet and sending the results of that query to `Remove-AzureVM` for deletion.

In Example 7-19, `Get-AzureVM` is passed the cloud service name and returns the properties of all the virtual machines in the cloud service as an array of configuration objects. Each result in the array is passed to the pipeline separately, so `Remove-AzureVM` is called for each virtual machine. The end result is that all of the virtual machines in the cloud service are deleted. The cloud service itself continues to exist.

Example 7-19. Deleting virtual machines using the PowerShell pipeline

```
Get-AzureVM -ServiceName $serviceName |
    Remove-AzureVM -DeleteVHD
```

Since the output of `Get-AzureVM` is written to the PowerShell pipeline, you can modify it by using other PowerShell cmdlets. In Example 7-20, I have added a call to the `where` command so that only virtual machines in the cloud service that start with the name `iis` will be deleted.

Example 7-20. Filtering the deletion of virtual machines

```
Get-AzureVM -ServiceName $serviceName |
    Where { $_.Name -like 'iis*'} |
    Remove-AzureVM -DeleteVHD
```

Optional—validate what you are deleting
When operating on virtual machines in a batch like this, it is advisable to validate what is being returned before executing the final command. In the preceding example, simply remove the final pipe | and the call to `Remove-AzureVM` to validate which virtual machines are being returned before the final delete.

The other method of deleting virtual machines is to delete the cloud service in which they are hosted. This technique has the advantage of cleaning up all of the virtual machines—and optionally their disks—along with the cloud service itself in one call to the API (see Example 7-21).

Example 7-21. Deleting all virtual machines by deleting the cloud service

```
Remove-AzureService $serviceName -DeleteAll
```

Optional—use -DeleteAll to delete all disks

Using the -DeleteAll parameter is equivalent to passing the -DeleteVHD parameter to Remove-AzureVM. The underlying disks, including the VHDs, will be deleted with the virtual machine.

Importing and Exporting Virtual Machine Configurations

Another set of cmdlets that can be very useful in certain situations are the Import-AzureVM and Export-AzureVM cmdlets. Using the Export-AzureVM cmdlet, you can save the configuration of a virtual machine to disk as an XML file. The Import-AzureVM cmdlet can be used to restore the configuration back into an object usable by PowerShell.

There are several use cases for these cmdlets:

- Moving a virtual machine from one cloud service to another
- Moving a virtual machine into or out of a virtual network
- Moving a virtual machine between subscriptions or regions

The last use case requires quite a bit more effort than the first two.

To demonstrate how these cmdlets work in more detail, I will walk you through exporting a virtual machine configuration, removing the virtual machine, and then re-creating it from the configuration in a new cloud service.

In Example 7-22, the Export-AzureVM cmdlet exports the configuration to the *C: \Scripts* folder. Feel free to place it wherever you want.

Example 7-22. Exporting a virtual machine configuration (Console pane)

```
$serviceName = "[cloud service name]"
$vmName = "ps-vm1"
$localPath = "C:\Scripts\$vmName.xml"

Export-AzureVM -ServiceName $serviceName -Name $vmName -Path $localPath
```

When the cmdlet has executed, you can open the file up directly in Notepad or an XML editor to view the contents. You should see the network endpoint configuration, and references to the disk names and their associated cache settings.

To import the virtual machine configuration and then re-create it, you first need to delete the virtual machine (see Example 7-23).

Example 7-23. Removing the virtual machine (Console pane)

```
Remove-AzureVM -ServiceName $serviceName -Name $vmName
```

Do not delete disks

When you use the `Import-AzureVM` and `Export-AzureVM` cmdlets, it is important to remember that the configuration references existing disks. If you delete the disks when deleting the virtual machine, you will no longer be able to import the virtual machine configuration.

Example 7-24 shows how you can import the configuration from the saved path. When the configuration is loaded, you can treat it just like you would a virtual machine configuration created from the `New-AzureVMConfig` cmdlet. The following code simply passes the `$vmConfig` to `New-AzureVM` for it to be re-created in a new cloud service. You could easily specify a virtual network here and migrate the virtual machine to the virtual network.

Example 7-24. Importing the virtual machine configuration (Console pane)

```
# Specify a new cloud service name
$newServiceName = "[new cloud service name]"

# The region for the new virtual machine must be the same as the disk location
$location = "[region name]"

# Load the configuration
$vmConfig = Import-AzureVM -Path $localPath

# Create the virtual machine using the imported configuration
$vmConfig | New-AzureVM -ServiceName $newServiceName -Location $location
```

The use case I mentioned about moving virtual machines between regions or subscriptions is relatively complicated but entirely doable in conjunction with the async blob copy cmdlet `Start-AzureStorageBlobCopy`.

Here is the general flow of how you could build a solution yourself:

1. Export the existing configuration for the virtual machine.
2. Copy the VHDs from the source subscription to the destination subscription (use `Select-AzureSubscription` to switch).
3. Register the copied VHDs in the destination subscription with `Add-AzureDisk` using the same disk names as the source.
4. Import the existing configuration files and create the virtual machine in a new cloud service.

A complete example (*http://bit.ly/copy_virtual_machine*) is posted in the TechNet Script Center for reference.

Summary and Conclusion

In this final chapter we have put all of the pieces of the puzzle together with virtual machines and PowerShell. We have learned how to use the advanced provisioning capabilities of the platform for Windows-based virtual machines and we have even learned how to deploy Linux virtual machines complete with enabled SSH authentication.

We have also explored some advanced management techniques such as executing scripts and entering PowerShell sessions remotely, along with using the custom script extension to execute scripts at boot time to customize your virtual machines. Finally, we covered some tips and tricks for deleting virtual machines and using the configuration import/export abilities to move virtual machines around in, and even out of, your subscription.

I hope you have learned some valuable techniques, tips, and tricks to help you with your automation and configuration tasks with Azure Infrastructure Services. You should now have a new tool in your toolbox that can help with most problems or challenges with your virtual machine and virtual network deployments, even if you are just using the Azure cmdlets when they are required or as part of a larger automation framework.

Index

Symbols
.publishsettings file, 6
  importing, 7

A
access control lists (ACL), 45–48
  adding/updating, 46–48
  managing, 142
  rules for, 45
access extension, 149
account names, 16
  creating VMs from OS disk and, 82
  creating VMs from VM images and, 82
Active Directory, 143
Add-AzureAccount cmdlet, 8
Add-AzureDataDisk cmdlet, 23
administrator accounts, 20
Amazon, 1
authenticating, 6–7
  in Linux, 136
  load balancer and, 42
  VHD uploads, 56
  with a certificate, 6
  with PowerShell, 7
availability sets, 136–140
  provisioning virtual machines in, 138
Azure PowerShell
  capturing VM image with, 70

environments, setting up, 5–10
subscriptions, 8–10
subscriptions, managing, 8–10

B
BgInfo extension, 149
BGP routing example, 129
billing
  cloud services, 34
  ExpressRoute, 128
blob data, 87–96
  asynchronous copy, 90–96
  managing, 87–90

C
cache, specifying, 80–81
certificates
  configuring for PowerShell Remote, 144–146
  deploying, 141
  managing manually, 10
cloud service conflicts, 28
cloud services
  billing, 34
  deploying applications to, 2
  virtual machines and, 19
cmdlets, 1
  development history of, 3
  open source nature of, 4

We'd like to hear your suggestions for improving our indexes. Send email to index@oreilly.com.

About the Author

Michael Washam is the CEO and cofounder of Opsgility (*http://www.opsgility.com*). Opsgility delivers instructor-led, remote-classroom, and on-demand training focused on Microsoft cloud technologies. Michael has extensive history in the IT industry, where he has worked as an IT professional, developer, evangelist, and program manager. While at Microsoft as a senior program manager on the Microsoft Azure runtime team, Michael led the release of the Microsoft Azure PowerShell cmdlets for compute and the Microsoft Azure SDK (runtime). As a senior technical evangelist, Michael worked on the initial Microsoft Azure Infrastructure-as-a-Service launch. In this role, Michael also shipped the IaaS Microsoft Azure training kit, and the Microsoft Azure PowerShell cmdlets for IaaS and cloud services.

Michael is a globally recognized speaker at conferences such as BUILD and TechEd, and an avid blogger, speaker, and trainer on cloud computing, debugging, and DevOps.

Colophon

The animal on the cover of *Automating Microsoft Azure Infrastructure Services* is a saltwater crocodile (*Crocodylus porosus*), the largest of all living reptiles. Found near the coast of Southeast Asia and northern Australia, a great deal of the cold-blooded saltwater crocodile's life is spent regulating the temperature of its very large body. If too cold, it will bask on rocks in the sun; if too warm, it submerges most of its body in the water to cool off. Though *salties*, as they are also called, can be found making this movement between saltwater sea and land, they are also often found in the fresh or brackish water of swamps, estuaries, and rivers.

Saltwater crocodiles are *apex predators* in their environment, meaning they have no natural predators of their own. They are not picky eaters, catching various fish, invertebrates, birds, or small mammals as opportunities arise. Cooling itself off underwater, the saltie finds opportunities to hunt in abundance: beginning with only its eyes and nostrils above water, the croc makes a powerful lunge into the air after prey that may venture near, usually killing its target with a snap of the jaws.

Crocodile species possess an incomparably strong bite due to large, very hard muscles on either side of a croc's jaw. In fact, scientists estimate the bite force of extinct species such as dinosaurs against that of modern crocodiles. However, though crocodile jaw muscles are optimally arranged for clamping down on prey, the corresponding muscles to open the mouth are weak—a few layers of duct tape suffice to keep the jaws closed.

Many of the animals on O'Reilly covers are endangered; all of them are important to the world. To learn more about how you can help, go to *animals.oreilly.com*.

The cover image is from *Meyers Kleines Lexicon*. The cover fonts are URW Typewriter and Guardian Sans. The text font is Adobe Minion Pro; the heading font is Adobe Myriad Condensed; and the code font is Dalton Maag's Ubuntu Mono.

Get even more for your money.

Join the O'Reilly Community, and register the O'Reilly books you own. It's free, and you'll get:

- $4.99 ebook upgrade offer
- 40% upgrade offer on O'Reilly print books
- Membership discounts on books and events
- Free lifetime updates to ebooks and videos
- Multiple ebook formats, DRM FREE
- Participation in the O'Reilly community
- Newsletters
- Account management
- 100% Satisfaction Guarantee

Signing up is easy:

1. Go to: oreilly.com/go/register
2. Create an O'Reilly login.
3. Provide your address.
4. Register your books.

Note: English-language books only

To order books online:
oreilly.com/store

For questions about products or an order:
orders@oreilly.com

To sign up to get topic-specific email announcements and/or news about upcoming books, conferences, special offers, and new technologies:
elists@oreilly.com

For technical questions about book content:
booktech@oreilly.com

To submit new book proposals to our editors:
proposals@oreilly.com

O'Reilly books are available in multiple DRM-free ebook formats. For more information:
oreilly.com/ebooks

Lightning Source UK Ltd.
Milton Keynes UK
UKOW05f0413281115

263630UK00012B/76/P